My rich dad said, "The richest people in the world look for and build networks, everyone else looks for work."

— *Robert T. Kiyosaki*
Author of the #1 New York Times Bestseller, Rich Dad Poor Dad & of the Rich Dad Book Series

Rich Dad's™ *Classics*

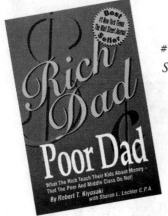

#1 *New York Times,* #1 *Wall Street Journal,*
#1 *Business Week,* #1 *Publishers Weekly,* as well as a
San Francisco Chronicle and *USA Today* bestseller.
Also featured on the bestseller lists of
*Amazon.com, Amazon.com UK and Germany,
E-trade.com, Sydney Morning Herald* (Australia),
Sun Herald (Australia), *Business Review Weekly*
(Australia), *Borders Books and Music* (U.S. and
Singapore), *Barnes & Noble.com.*

*Wall Street Journal, The New York Times
Business* and *Business Week* bestseller.
Also featured on the bestseller lists of the
Sydney Morning Herald (Australia), *Sun
Herald* (Australia), *Business Review Weekly*
(Australia), *Amazon.com, Barnes &
Noble.com, Borders Books and Music*
(U.S. and Singapore).

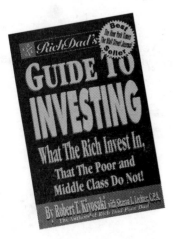

*USA Today, Wall Street Journal, The New York
Times Business, Business Week* and *Publishers
Weekly* bestseller.

Wall Street Journal, The New York Times,
and *USA Today* bestsellers.

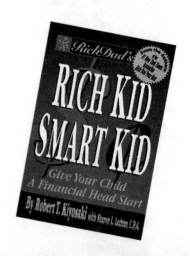

THE BUSINESS SCHOOL FOR PEOPLE WHO LIKE HELPING PEOPLE

By Robert T. Kiyosaki

with Sharon L. Lechter, C.P.A.

Copyright © 2001 by Robert T. Kiyosaki and Sharon L. Lechter
All rights reserved.

Published by TechPress, Inc. in association with
CASHFLOW Technologies, Inc.

"CASHFLOW" and Rich Dad are trademarks of
CASHFLOW Technologies, Inc.

 are trademarks of
CASHFLOW Technologies, Inc.

Tech Press, Inc., 4330 N. Civic Center Plaza, Suite 101, Scottsdale, AZ 85251

Visit our Web site at www.richdad.com

Printed in the United States of America

First TechPress, Inc. Printing: March 2001

10 9 8 7 6 5 4 3 2 1

Designed by Imagesupport.com, llc
Scottsdale, Arizona

THE BUSINESS SCHOOL FOR PEOPLE WHO LIKE HELPING PEOPLE

Introduction

Robert Kiyosaki, author of the bestsellers *Rich Dad Poor Dad, Rich Dad's CASHFLOW Quadrant, Rich Dad's Guide to Investing* and *Rich Kid, Smart Kid* is an internationally recognized speaker and teacher on the subject of money. J.P. Morgan declared *"Rich Dad Poor Dad* a must read for millionaires" as reported in *the Wall Street Journal,* and *USA Today* called *Rich Dad Poor Dad* "a starting point for anyone looking to gain control of their financial future."

Robert often says, "We go to school to learn to work hard for money. I write books and create products that teach people how to have money work hard for them...so they can enjoy the luxuries of this great world we live in." Robert's books and financial board games *CASHFLOW 101, 202* and *CASHFLOW for KIDS* have been phenomenally successful. *Rich Dad Poor Dad* is now available in over 35 languages. Robert credits this success, in part, to the network marketing industry. "While we did not target the network marketing industry, it has been incredibly supportive and applauds our message that people need to take control of their own financial future."

While Robert does not endorse any specific network marketing organization, he recognizes the value of the opportunities offered by the industry and highlights those values in this booklet, *The Business School for People Who Like Helping People.*

"Never before has it been so easy to become rich," Robert says. "It took me over 30 years and two business failures to gain the education and experience needed to build a successful business. The network marketing industry offers a ready-made business system to anyone wanting to take control of his or her financial future.

"My rich dad taught me that one of the most powerful words in the world of business is 'network.' He said, 'The richest people in the world look for and build networks; everyone else looks for work. You can have the greatest idea or product, but it will only be successful if you have a network to tell people about it and a network of distribution to sell it through.'"

Many organizations in the network marketing industry today are trying to distance themselves from the term "network marketing" because they believe it to have a negative connotation. In contrast, Robert emphasizes the word "network" as the true key to financial success.

In his second book of the Rich Dad series, *Rich Dad's CASHFLOW Quadrant*, Robert describes the four types of people who make up the world of business and the core value differences

between them.

The *E* stands for "employee." The *S* stands for "self-employed" or "small business owner." The B stands for "business owner" and the *I* stands for "investor". These four quadrants represent how people make their money.

Traditional schools train you for the left side of the Quadrant, to be employees or self-employed individuals, where you learn how to work hard for money. Robert Kiyosaki's books and games train you for the right side of the Quadrant, to be business owners and investors where your business and money work hard for you. Robert supports the network marketing industry because it assists you in building a "B" business on the right side of the Quadrant.

In reviewing the Quadrant, Robert points out that on the left side of the Quadrant, employees and self-employed individuals represent earning money on their own, as individual's. This means their income potential is finite, limited to their own ability and their personal time to perform. There are only so many hours in a day. However, successful people on the right side of the Quadrant operate as a team. They form their own networks for success. Their income potential is infinite because it is based on other

Work

Individuals
Income Potential is Finite

Network

Operates as a Team
Income Potential is Infinite

people's time and other people's money working for them.

Let's review the word "network." Think of some of the most successful businesses you know and evaluate how their success is due to their network of customers, salespeople, suppliers, etc. We call national television stations, television networks. The Internet is called a network.

The key to your financial success may be through finding or building a network.

NETWORK 1

Why Do You Recommend the Business?

I am often asked, "Since you did not become rich from a network marketing business, why do you recommend that others get into the business?"

There are several reasons I recommend the industry, and they will be explained in this booklet.

The Closing of My Mind

It was sometime during the mid-1970s a friend asked me to a presentation on a new business opportunity. Being a person who makes it a habit of regularly investigating business and investment opportunities, I agreed to attend the meeting. Although I thought it strange that the business meeting was to be held at a private home rather than in an office, I went along anyway. That meeting was to be my introduction to the world of network marketing.

Leaving the three-hour presentation, my friend asked me what I thought of the business opportunity presented. My reply was, "It was interesting but not for me."

When my friend asked me why I was not interested, I said, "I am already building my own business. Why do I need to build a business with other people?" I then said, "Besides, I have heard rumors that these network marketing businesses are just pyramid schemes and are illegal." Before my friend could say anything further, I walked off into the night, got into my car, and drove away. My mind was closed and I did not want to hear anymore. It would be years before it would open again...open enough to listen and to begin to change my opinion about the industry.

At that stage of my life in the mid-1970s, I was building my first international business. So I was very busy anyway keeping my daytime job and building this business in my spare time. The business I was building was a manufacturing and marketing business focused on bringing to market the first nylon and Velcro surfer wallets. Soon after my first network marketing meeting, my sports wallet business boomed. My two years of hard work was paying off. Success, fame, and fortune seemed to pour down upon my two partners and me. We had reached our goal, which was to become millionaires before we were 30, and in the 1970s, a million dollars was worth something. My company and my products were written about in such magazines as *Surfer, Runner's World,* and *Gentleman's Quarterly.* We were the hot new products in the sporting goods world, and business poured in from all over the world. My first international business was up and running and I did not think about the network marketing industry again for 15 years.

A Change of Mind

Sometime in the early 1990s a friend I respect for his financial wisdom and his business success told me he was in the network marketing business. Bill was already very wealthy from his real estate investments, so it puzzled me why he would be in network marketing. Now curious, I asked him, "Why are you in the business? You don't need the money, do you?"

Laughing out loud, Bill said, "You know I like making money, but I am not in the business because I need the money. My finances are in great shape."

I knew that Bill had just completed commercial real estate projects worth over a billion dollars in the last two years, so I also knew he was doing well. Yet his vague answer made me more curious, so I pressed on, asking him, "So why are you in a network marketing business?"

"It's called a 'consumer distribution business.'" He replied. "We don't call it network marketing anymore."

"Whatever," I replied. "Whatever you call it, tell me why *you* of all people are in such a business?"

Bill thought for a long while and then began speaking in his slow Texas style. "For years, people have asked me for real estate investment tips. They want to know how to become rich by investing in real estate. Many want to know if they can invest with me, or how they can find real estate for no money down."

Nodding in agreement, I said, "I am asked the same questions."

"The problem is…,"said Bill continuing on, "most cannot invest with me because they do not have enough money to qualify for my investments. And the reason they often want a no-money-down deal is because they don't have any money. Either they don't have enough money to get into one of my deals, or they don't have any money to put down."

"You mean they don't have any money, or if they do have money, they don't have enough money for you to help them. They aren't rich enough for your investments?" I said.

Bill nodded. "And on top of that, if they do have a little money, it is their life savings and they are often very afraid of losing the money they do have. And you and I know that a person who is afraid of losing, often loses."

My conversation with Bill went on for a few more minutes, but I soon had to dash for the airport. I was still not sure why he was in a network marketing business, but my closed mind was beginning to open. I was beginning to want to know why he was in the network marketing business, or consumer distribution business, as he called it.

Over the next few months, my dialogue with Bill continued. Slowly I began to understand his reasons for being in the business. His primary reasons were:

1. **He wanted to help people.** This was his main reason for being in the business. Although a very rich man, he was not a greedy or arrogant man.

2. **He wanted to help himself.** "You have to be rich to invest with me. I realized that if I helped more people become rich, then I would have more investors." Bill continued,

"The irony is that the more I helped others become rich building their own business, the more my business grew...and I became richer. Now I have a thriving consumer distribution business, more investors, and more money of my own to invest with. Talk about win-win. That is why in the last few years, I have begun investing in much larger real estate projects. As you know, it's hard to get really rich investing in small real estate deals. It can be done, but if you don't have much money, all you get are the real estate deals that people with money don't want."

3. **He loves teaching and learning.** "I love working with people who want to learn. It is exhausting working with people who think they know everything, and in my world of real estate investing, I work with many of those people. It is tough working with someone who knows all the answers. For me, people who come to network marketing are looking for new answers and are ready to learn. I love teaching, learning, and sharing new ideas with people excited about their on going education. As you know, I have a degree in accounting and an MBA in finance. This business gives me a chance to teach others what I know and continue learning along with everyone else. You'd be surprised how many very smart, well-educated people from different backgrounds are in this business. There are also many people without a formal education who are in the business to gain the education they need to find financial security in a world with less and less job security. We get together and share what we already know from our life's experiences and what we are learning. I love teaching and I love learning, and that is why I love this business. It's a great business and a great *real-life* business school."

An Open Mind

So sometime during the early 1990s my mind began to open and my point of view on the industry began to change. I began to see things that my closed mind could not see. I began to see things that were good and positive about the industry rather than the things that were negative...and there are negatives to the industry. But then again, there is something negative about most things.

After retiring in 1994, financially free at the age of 47, I began my own research into the network marketing industry. Anytime someone invited me to one of his or her presentations, I went along, just to listen to what he or she had to say. I did join a few of the companies if I liked what they said. But I joined not necessarily to make more money; I joined to take a long hard look at the positives and the negatives of each business. Instead of just closing my mind, I wanted to find my own answers. After looking into several businesses, I saw the negatives that most people see at first glance, such as the strange people who initially come into the business and promote the business. It is true that many dreamers, hustlers, con men, losers, and get-rich-quick artists are attracted to these businesses. One of the challenges of a network marketing business is that they have an open door policy, which allows almost anyone to join. This open-door policy is the *fair and equal opportunity* that most socialists cry out for, yet I did not meet any hard-core socialists in these businesses. These businesses are for capitalists or at least for people who hope to become capitalists.

After getting through the masses of wannabes, hustlers, and dreamers, I finally began meeting the leaders of some of the businesses. The ones I met were some of the most intelligent, kind, ethical, moral, and professional people I have met in all my years of business. Once I got over my own prejudices and met people I respected and related to, I found the heart of the industry. I could now see what I could not see before. I could now see the good *and* the bad.

So this booklet is written to answer the question, "Since you did not become rich from a network marketing business, why do you recommend that others get into the business?" It is because I **did not** gain my fortune from the network marketing business that I can be a bit more objective about the industry. This brief booklet describes what I see as the **real** value of a network marketing business...a value that goes beyond just the potential of making a lot of money.

As my rich dad said, "The richest people in the world look for, and build networks, everyone else looks for work."

While a network marketing business **is not** for everyone, the industry continues to grow as a powerful financial force in the world today. People concerned about doing business in the future and about their own personal financial future should take an objective look at the industry.

Value #1: Life-Changing Business Education

It's Not the Money

"We have the best compensation plan." I often heard this comment when I was investigating different network marketing companies. The people anxious to show me their business opportunity would tell me stories of people making hundreds of thousands of dollars a month because of the business. I have also met people who really do make hundreds of thousands of dollars a month from their network marketing business...so I do not doubt the massive earning potential of network marketing.

The lure of making a lot of money draws many people into the business. Yet I do not recommend looking into a network marketing business primarily for the money.

It's Not the Products

"We have the best products." This statement is the second most emphasized benefit I was presented with when inspecting different network marketing businesses. In my investigating the different network marketing companies, I was taken by complete surprise by how many different products or services are delivered via a network marketing system.

The first network marketing business opportunity I looked into in the 1970s sold vitamins. I tried them and found them to be excellent quality vitamins. I still take some of those vitamins today. As my search went on, I found network marketing businesses in these main stream product lines:

1. Consumable home care products
2. Telephone services
3. Real estate
4. Financial services
5. Internet Websites
6. Internet market distribution, selling at discount just about everything that Wal-Mart and K-Mart sell
7. Health care products
8. Jewelry
9. Tax services
10. Educational toys

And the list goes on. At least once a month, I hear about a new network marketing company with a new twist on products or on their compensation plan. I join some of them because I want the product or service they offer. But product or compensation plans are not the main reason I encourage people to look into different network marketing businesses.

It's the Education Plan

The number one reason I recommend a network marketing business is for its system of education. The job you have is to invest the time to look past the compensation and products and really look into the heart of the company to see if it is truly interested in training and educating you. That takes more time than just listening to a three-hour sales pitch and looking at colorful product catalogues. To find out how good their education really is may require you to get off your couch and invest some time going to their training and education functions. If you like what you hear from the initial presentation, take some time to actually meet the people who do the educating and training. That is what I did, and what I found impressed me.

Look carefully, because most network marketing companies say they have great education plans. Yet I found that many *did not* have the great education and training systems they claimed they did. In most companies I looked into, the only training they had was a recommended book list, and then they focused on training you to recruit your friends and family into the business. In other words, all they educated you into becoming was a better salesperson for their products or their system. So take your time and look carefully, because there are many network marketing companies that do have excellent education and training plans...in my opinion, some of the best real-life business training I have seen anywhere.

What to Look For in an Education Plan

If you have read my other books, you already know that I come from a family of educators. My dad was the head of the school systems for the State of Hawaii. Yet although I came from a family of educators, I did not like traditional education. Although I received a Congressional Appointment to a prominent federal military academy in New York and graduated with my Bachelor of Science degree, the traditional world of education bored me. I went through the motions of being a student and graduated, but rarely was I challenged or interested in what I was required to study.

After graduating from school, I joined the U.S. Marine Corps and was accepted into the U.S. Navy Flight Program at Pensacola, Florida. The Vietnam War was on and there was an urgent need to train more pilots. While a student pilot, I found the type of education that excited and challenged me. Most of us have heard the overused cliché, "turning caterpillars into butterflies." Well in flight school, that is exactly what they do. When I entered flight school, I was already a commissioned officer, having graduated from a military academy. But many of the students entering flight school were fresh from civilian colleges and did resemble caterpillars. Being the era of the hippies, there were some very strange characters standing there in their civilian clothes, ready to begin a *life-changing educational program.* If they survived the training, two to three years later, they would emerge as butterflies, i.e. pilots ready to take on the rigors of some of the toughest flying in the world.

The movie *Top Gun*, starring Tom Cruise, was about the best of the *caterpillars* that became *butterflies*. Just before going to

Vietnam, I too was stationed in San Diego, California, where the Top Gun school is located. Although I was not a good enough pilot to be considered for that prestigious school, the energy and confidence displayed by the young pilots in the movie was the way most of us felt as we prepared to go to war. We changed from scruffy young men who could not fly...to being young men who were trained and ready to face challenges most people would rather avoid. The change I observed in myself and in my fellow student pilots is what I mean when I say "life-changing education." Once I finished flight school and left for Vietnam, my life was never the same. I was not the same person who entered flight school.

Years after flight school, many of my fellow pilots went on to become very successful in the world of business. When we get together and re-tell old war stories, we often remark that it was the training we received in flight school that had a tremendous impact on our business success today.

So when I speak of *Life-changing business education*, I speak of education powerful enough to change a caterpillar into a butterfly. When you look into the educational plan of a network marketing business, I recommend an educational plan that has the power to make that much of a difference in your life.

Yet I caution you, just as in flight school, not everyone makes it through the program.

Real Life Business School

One of the best things about flight school was that pilots just returning from the war in Vietnam trained us. When they spoke to us, they spoke to us from real life experience. One of the problems I had in business school was that many of the teachers had no real, life business experience. In network marketing, the people at the top who teach have to be successful in the real world, or they would not be at the top. In the world of traditional business schools, you do not have to be successful in the real world of business to teach business. That may be why the instructors in the traditional world of business education do not earn as much as some of the instructors in the world of network marketing education.

So when looking into a network marketing business, seek out

the people at the top, the people who are successful in the business and then ask yourself if you want to learn from them.

Some of the more important real-life business subjects network marketing companies teach are:

1. An attitude of success
2. Leadership skills
3. Communication skills
4. People skills
5. Overcoming personal fears, doubts, and lack of confidence
6. Overcoming the fear of rejection
7. Money management skills
8. Investing skills
9. Accountability skills
10. Time management skills
11. Goal setting
12. Systemization

The successful people I have met in the network marketing business have developed these skills from the network marketing training programs. Regardless if you reach the top of the network marketing system or make much money, the training is of great value for the rest of your life. If the educational plan is good, it can improve your life for the better, maybe forever.

What Is Life-Changing Education?

The following is the diagram I created to explain what I mean by life-changing education. Notice that it is a tetrahedron, which means a four-sided polyhedron, more commonly known as a pyramid...and the pyramids of Egypt have survived for centuries. In other words, tetrahedrons or pyramids are very stable structures. Scholars have believed for centuries that universal law or nature operates in fours, in this case four sides. That is why there are the four seasons, which are winter, spring, summer, fall. For those who study astrology, there are four primary signs, which are earth, wind, fire, and water. When I speak of life-changing education, the changes are again found in the number four. In other words, for true life-changing education to be effective, it must affect all four points of the Learning Pyramid.

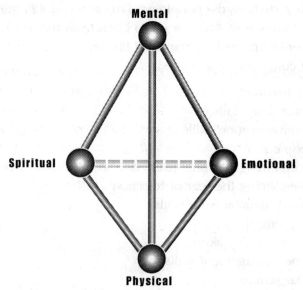

Traditional education focuses primarily on mental education. It teaches you skills such as reading, writing, and arithmetic, all very important skills. These are often called *cognitive skills*. What I personally did not like about traditional education was how it impacted the emotional, physical, and spiritual aspects of education. I will discuss each point individually.

1. **Emotional Education:** One of my complaints about traditional education is that it preys on the emotion of fear...more specifically, the fear of making mistakes, which leads to the fear of failing. Instead of inspiring me to learn, the teacher used the fear of failure to motivate me, saying such things as, "If you don't get good grades, you won't get a high-paying job."

   Also, when I was in school, I was punished for making mistakes. In school I emotionally learned to fear making mistakes. The problem is, in the real world, the people who get ahead are the people who make the most mistakes and learn from them.

   My poor dad, the schoolteacher, thought making a mistake was a sin. My rich dad, on the other hand, said, "Making mistakes is how we are designed to learn. We learn to ride a bicycle by falling off and getting back on again, falling off and getting back on." He also said, "It is a sin to make a mistake and not learn from it."

Explaining further, he said, "The reason so many people lie after making a mistake is because they are emotionally terrified of admitting they made a mistake...hence they waste an opportunity to learn and grow. Making a mistake, admitting it without blaming your mistake on someone else, or justifying, or making excuses, is how we learn. Making a mistake and not admitting it, or blaming someone else for your mistakes, is a sin."

In the world of traditional business, the same attitude toward mistakes prevails. In the world of business, if you make a mistake you are often fired or punished. In the world of network marketing, you are encouraged to learn by making mistakes, correcting, and getting smarter mentally as well as emotionally. When I was learning to sell in the corporate world, the sales people who underachieved were fired. In the world of network marketing, the leader's focus is to work with those who are not doing well and to encourage them to move up, not to fire them. You would probably never have learned to ride a bicycle if you were punished for falling off and given a failing grade in bicycle riding.

I believe that I am more successful financially than most people because I failed more than most people. In other words, I got ahead because I made more mistakes than people who learned that making mistakes was bad or meant they were stupid. In network marketing, you are encouraged to make mistakes, correct, learn, and grow. To me, that is life-changing education...education that is almost the opposite of traditional education.

If you are terrified of making mistakes and afraid of failing, the network marketing business is especially good for you. I have witnessed network marketing training programs that build and restore a person's self-confidence...and once you have more confidence, your life is changed forever.

2. **Physical Education:** Simply put, people afraid of making mistakes don't learn much because they don't do much. Most people know that learning is really a physical process as much as it is a mental process. Reading and writing are physical processes, just as learning to play tennis is a physical process. If you have been conditioned to know all the right answers and not to make mistakes, the chances are your educational process is hampered. How can you progress if you know all the answers but are terrified of trying anything?

The network marketing companies I have studied all encourage *physical learning* as much as they encourage *mental learning*. They encourage you to go out and face your fears by taking action, making a mistake, learning from the mistake, and growing mentally, emotionally, and physically stronger from the process.

Traditional education encourages you to learn the facts and then emotionally teaches you to be afraid of making mistakes, which holds you back physically. Living in an environment of fear is not healthy, mentally, emotionally, physically, or financially. As I have stated before, I have more money not because I am academically smarter, but because I made more mistakes, admitted to making the mistake, and learned my lessons from the mistakes. I then went on to make more mistakes....and I am looking forward ton making more mistakes in the future...while most people are working hard to make no more mistakes in their future....which is why we have different futures. You cannot improve your future if you are not willing to try something new and risk making mistakes and learning from them.

The best network marketing companies encourage their people to learn something new mentally, take action, make mistakes, learn, correct, and repeat the process. That is real-life education.

If you are afraid of making mistakes, but know you need to

make some changes in your life, then a good network marketing program could be the best long-term personal development program for you. A good network marketing company will take you by the hand and guide you to a life beyond fear and failing. And if you don't want your hand held, they won't hold it.

3. **Spiritual Education:** First of all, I feel it important that I explain my personal views before going into this often hot and emotional topic. I use the word *spiritual* versus *religious* for specific reasons. Just as there are good network marketing companies and bad network marketing companies, in my opinion there are good religious organizations and bad religious organizations. More specifically, I have seen religious organizations strengthen a person spiritually, and I have seen other religious organizations weaken a person spiritually.

   So when I speak of spiritual education, it may include religious education or it may not. When I speak of spiritual education, I speak non-denominationally. When it comes to religion, I support the Constitution of the United States, which grants the freedom of religious choice.

   The reason I am cautious about this subject is because I was told at an early age, "Never discuss religion, politics, sex, and money." And I agree with that statement simply because these subjects can be volatile and emotional. It is not my intent to offend your personal feelings or beliefs but to support your rights to have them.

Beyond Human Limitations

When I speak of a person's spirit, I speak of the power that propels us past our mental, emotional, and physical limitations...limitations that often define our human condition.

While I was in Vietnam, I witnessed young men who were wounded and knew they were dying, yet they continued to fight on so others could live. A classmate from elementary school who fought behind enemy lines for most of his time in Vietnam said it most accurately when he said, "I am alive today because dead men kept fighting." He went on to say, "Twice I was in battles where I was the only one to come out alive. Your life changes when you realize that your friends gave their lives so that you could live."

Many nights before a battle, I would sit at the bow of the aircraft carrier silently as the waves passed below. In these long moments of silence I made peace with my soul. I realized that in the morning, I would face death again. It was during one of these long evenings of quiet and solitude that I realized that to die the next day was the easy way out. I realized that living was in many ways much harder than dying. Once I was at peace with the possibility of either life or death, I could then choose how I wanted to live my life the next day. In other words, would I fly with courage or would I fly with fear? Once I made my choice, I called on my human spirit to carry me through the next day, to fly and fight to the best of my ability, regardless of the final outcome.

War is a horrible event. It causes people to do horrible things to other human beings. Yet, it was in war that I also saw the very best of humanity. It was in war that I gained a sense of human power far beyond our human limitations. And we all have it. I know you have it.

The good news is that you don't have to go to war to witness this power. One day while watching a track meet of physically challenged young girls and boys, I witnessed and was touched by the same human spirit. When I saw young people, some without legs, sprinting with prosthetic legs, running with all their heart and soul during a 100-yard dash, their spirit touched my spirit. Tears came to my eyes as I watched one young girl, with only one leg, running with all her heart. I could see on her face the pain caused by running on her replacement leg, yet her physical pain was no match for the power of her spirit. Although she did not win the race, she won my heart. She touched my human spirit and reminded me of what I had forgotten. At that moment, I realized that all these young people were running for all of us as much as they were running for themselves. They ran to remind us of the potential power we all have stored inside us.

We see great human spirit in movies. In the movie *Brave Heart,* Mel Gibson rides in front of his ragtag band of Scottish farmers, terrified by the powerful British Army in front of them, and bellows from his soul, "They can kill our bodies, but they can't take our freedom." At that moment, he is speaking from his human spirit to theirs. By touching their spirits, he was overpowering their emotions of fear and doubt, caused by lack of training and inferior weapons. He ignited their spirits to go on and defeat the most powerful army in the world.

I have noticed that the successful leaders in network marketing have been trained to develop this ability to speak to the human spirit. They have the ability to touch the greatness in those coming behind them and to inspire them to move up...to go beyond their human limitations. That is the power of life-changing education.

Looking at the diagram of the Learning Pyramid, you can see what happens when people are moved by their spirit and not emotionally or mentally.

Communicating Mentally

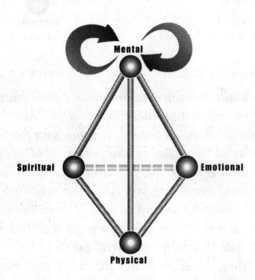

Generally nothing much happens if teaching is simply mental. We have all said things like, "I will begin losing weight next week." And then we continue to gain weight. Or we say such things as, "I will sell or recruit more next month." Or "I will begin saving money with the next pay check." The reason nothing changes is because it is only a mental activity. In most cases, real change requires all four points of the tetrahedron.

Communicating Emotionally

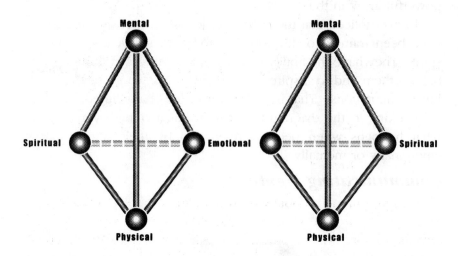

Note: Emotional communication is also called sentic communication. It means communicating emotions more than words. For example, we have all entered a room and felt someone who was angry at us even before the person said a word. Sentic communication is much like two tuning forks vibrating. If they are on the same frequency, you can hit one tuning fork, have it vibrate, and soon the second tuning fork will begin to vibrate. That means, when we are afraid, we often attract other fearful people or people that prey on fearful people. When I was a kid, we would often say such things as, "I get bad vibes from that guy." That is an example of sentic or emotional communication.

One of the great values of being trained by a network marketing company with a great education plan is that it encourages you to overcome your emotional limitations and speak from your human spirit.

Communicating Physically

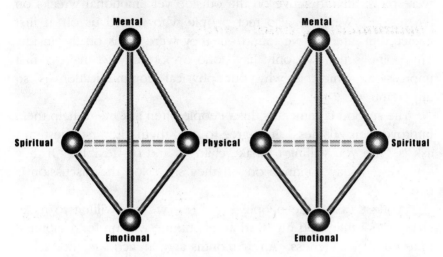

We have all met people who we are attracted to physically. We have also met people who we are repulsed by, just because of the way they look. The reason is, physical communication or visual communication, what a person looks like is, at first glance, the most powerful of all the communications.

Studies have shown that true person-to-person communication is made up of approximately:

10%	words
35%	emotions
50%	visual or physical
5%	other variables.

In other words, what you look like, or if you are frowning, slouching, dressed inappropriately, all impact your effectiveness in communication. Obviously these are rough estimates or approximations, yet they serve as good guidelines to improving communication between people.

The great network marketing companies spend a lot of time on improving a person's physical appearance. In one company, they even offered an optional weight loss and physical exercise program. The leaders know that healthy, physically attractive people communicate more effectively than unhealthy people.

I would like to make two comments on the subject of physical communication. The first comment is, we have all met people who were physically attractive on the outside yet emotional wrecks on the inside. We have also met people who turned us off at first glance, but later on we found out they were gems on the inside. The point is that we only have one opportunity to make a first impression, which is why our physical communication is so important.

The second comment is this. People often ask me to help them improve their business. If I agree to help them, the first question I ask is, "Are you willing to make changes and be flexible?" If they say "Yes," I may continue on. If they say "No," the discussion is over.

In most cases, the people say, "Yes, we are willing to make changes." I then nod my head and continue waiting for a moment to test their willingness. A few months ago, an acquaintance asked for help in improving the profitability of his business. I asked the same question about his willingness to make a change and he agreed. I immediately said, "Then the first step is please shave off your mustache."

Immediately the person balked and said, "I am not willing to shave off my mustache. I have had it since high school." The discussion was over and I did not work with him on improving his business. The point was not his mustache…but his willingness to change. I did not care if he kept his mustache or not. I was just testing his willingness to change. I could have done it with his tie, or his shoes, or anything physical. You see most people mentally want to change, as my friend did. But when I gave him the test of physically changing, he pulled back. All education is ultimately physical. If a person is not willing to learn physically, the chances of lasting educational change is minimal.

My rich dad used to say, "If you have three cats sitting on the fence, and two decide to jump off, how many cats are left?"

The answer is, "There are still three cats on the fence." The reason is that just *deciding* to jump does not mean any jumped off physically. And that is why my rich dad would say, "Tomorrow is the busiest day of the year." Most people find it easy to decide to improve their lives in some way, but then put off doing anything about it until tomorrow." My rich dad also said, "The problem is, most people ultimately run out of tomorrows." So the lesson is, most people want to change something in their lives, but change only begins when you finally take action...and that is why the physical aspect of education is so important.

The Best Education I Ever Had

Entering flight school right out of college was one of the smartest things I have done. It was not about learning to fly or preparing for war that was important. It was about preparing me for real life. I was no longer a child or school kid and the training I received was just what I needed at that time of my life. It was life-changing education because it changed me mentally, emotionally, physically, and spiritually. When I returned from the war, I had the confidence to take on the financial and business challenges that most people back down from.

If you are ready for some kind of change in your life, look into the educational programs offered by some of the network marketing companies. Take some time to see if the business, the compensation, the products, and the education are what you may need at this stage of your life. If you decide a company addresses each of these areas, then consider starting a part-time business with the company.

The rest of this booklet is about the other values I have found hidden in many network marketing companies.

Suggested Listening

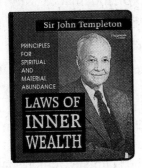

6 Audiocassettes/
Bonus Cassette
Laws of Inner Wealth
by Sir John Templeton

6 Audiocassettes/Workbook/
FREE Bonus Cassette
The 10 Qualities
of Charismatic
People by Tony Alessandra

Nightingale Conant

Value #2: The Value of Changing Quadrants...

instead of just changing jobs.

How many times have you heard people say some of the following statements?

1. "I wish I could quit my job."
2. "I'm tired of going from job to job."
3. "I wish I could make more money, but I can't afford to quit and start all over with a new company. And I don't want to go back to school and learn a new profession."
4. "Every time I get a pay raise, most of my raise is eaten up by taxes."
5. "I'm working hard, but the only people getting rich are the owners of the company."
6. "I'm working hard, but I'm not getting ahead financially. I've got to start thinking about retirement."
7. "I'm afraid technology or a younger worker will make me obsolete."
8. "I can't keep working this hard. I'm getting too old for this."
9. "I went to dental school to be a dentist, but I don't want to be a dentist anymore."
10. "I just want to do something different and meet new people.

I'm tired of wasting my time, hanging around people without much ambition and who aren't going anywhere. I'm tired of spending time with people who work just hard enough...so they won't be fired, and I'm also tired of working for a company that pays us just enough...so we won't quit."

These are often statements made by individuals trapped in one of the quadrants of the Cashflow Quadrant. These are comments often made by people ready to change quadrants. It may be time for them to move on.

What Is the CASHFLOW Quadrant?

My second book in the Rich Dad series is *Rich Dad's CASHFLOW Quadrant.* Many people say that it is my most important book because it is very eye-opening. I wrote the book for anyone who is ready to make a change in life...a change far greater than simply going from job to job.

The diagram below is my rich dad's Cashflow Quadrant.

The *E* stands for "employee."
The *S* stands for "self-employed" or "small business owner."
The *B* stands for "business owner."
The *I* stands for "investor."

The way you know which quadrant you are in is simply by which quadrant your cash flows from. In other words, if you receive your income from a job and you receive a regular paycheck from a company or business you do not own, then your cash flows out of the E quadrant. A person can be a janitor or the president of the company and be an employee. These people may think or say words such as, "I am looking for a safe, secure job with benefits." Or words such as, "How much do we get for overtime?" Or "How many paid holidays do we have?"

If you are on commission or charge for your work by the hour then you are probably in the S quadrant. Many times direct commission sales people such as real estate agents are from the S quadrant. These people may be heard saying words such as, "My usual commission is 6% of the total purchase price." The S quadrant may also include professional people such as lawyers and doctors. People who charge by the hour, are generally from the S quadrant. They may say, "My hourly rate is $50 per hour." Or they may say, "My fee will be $1000 for the job." The S quadrant also includes most small business owners, such as owners of restaurants, family businesses, consultants, service people such as yard and house cleaners. These people are often the rugged individuals who like doing things on their own. These people often give the advice, "Never work for someone else. You should work for yourself." Or, "If you want something done right, do it yourself."

If your income comes from a business that you do not have to work in, then you are in the B quadrant. If your income comes from investments, then you are in the I quadrant. If your income comes from company or government retirement plans, then chances are that is income from the E quadrant. It is also possible to receive income from more than one quadrant. For example, my wife and I receive income from all four quadrants...yet most of our income comes from our investments...so we say we operate out of the I quadrant.

For the most part, the definitions are simple and clear-cut. The two quadrants that often cause some confusion are the S and the B quadrants. I am often asked, "What is the difference between a self-employed or small business owner and a B or big business owner? The difference is easy to define.

My answer is, "A B or big business owner can leave his or her business for a year or more and come back to find it running better and even more profitably. A self-employed or small business owner often cannot afford to stay away for any length of time. In most cases, if a self-employed or small business owner stops working, his or her income stops coming in."

And that is the general difference between the S and the B quadrant. When people say, "I'm going to quit my job and go out on my own to do my own thing," most of these people move from the E to the S quadrant *rather than from* the E to the B quadrant. One of the reasons 9 out of 10 small businesses fail is simply because the S quadrant is the quadrant of very hard work. Many small businesses fail because of either financial exhaustion or physical exhaustion...or both. The S quadrant is where the small business owner is under pressure from customers, the government, and employees, if he or she has any. It's hard to do much productive work when you have so many people making demands on you at once.

The S quadrant can also stand for satisfaction...for it is in this quadrant that many people do what they truly love. The S quadrant is where people who *want to do their own thing*, often migrate. The sad news is that it is the quadrant that has some of the lowest paid people of all the quadrants. I recently saw an article that stated that many small businesses owners or independent contractors in America earn less than $25,000 a year. As stated earlier, the S quadrant is the quadrant that most businesses fail in. Many small businesses never even get off the ground.

What Do You Want to Be When You Grow Up?

When I was a kid, my poor dad often said, "Go to school, get good grades, so you can get a safe secure job." He was programming me for the E quadrant.

My mother often said, "If you want to be rich, you should become a doctor or lawyer. That way you'll always have a profession to fall back on." She was programming me for the S quadrant.

My rich dad said, "If you want to be rich...you should mind your own business." He went on to say, "Most people never become rich because they spend their lives minding someone else's business." He also said, "The more you seek job security, the less control you have over your life. Control over how much you earn, how much you pay in taxes, and control over your free time." My rich dad had a lot of free time simply because he owned businesses rather than worked for or in a business. He hired E and S quadrant people to run and manage his businesses for him. That is why he had so much free time and personal freedom and had more money, but legally paid less in taxes. He went on to say, "If you want to be free, then you'd better mind your own business." And the kind of business he was talking about was a business in the B quadrant, not the S quadrant.

In the book, *Rich Dad's CASHFLOW Quadrant*, I review my rich dad's beliefs around the word *control.* My rich dad often said, "The more you seek job security or become a licensed professional such as a doctor, lawyer, accountant, real estate broker, or stock broker, the more you give up control over your life. The more you give up control, the more you give up your freedom. That is why he said, "When someone asks you 'What do you want to be when you grow up?' Simply say, "I'm going to mind my own businesses." And he meant the B quadrant business, not the S quadrant.

How to Change Quadrants

After reading *Rich Dad's CASHFLOW Quadrant* and understanding what it takes to change quadrants, many people ask me, "How do I change quadrants? You make it sound easy, but for most of us, it isn't that easy."

My reply is, "Changing from the left side of the Quadrant, the E and S side, to the right side of the Quadrant, the B and I side, is easy for some people. Unfortunately, it was not easy for me. If not for my rich dad guiding me, I might not have made it." I go on to explain that I was born into a family of well-educated educators. In my family, a good education and a secure job or profession were very important core values. I say this because the change of quadrants may mean a shift away from family core values…and that is why it is not that easy for some people to change quadrants, even if they want to. From my mom and dad's point of view, the rich people who were business owners and investors were often considered greedy, evil, uncaring, and sometimes dishonest.

When my mom and dad found out that I wanted to enter the world of business instead of becoming a highly paid employee or professional person, they were disappointed in me. It went against their values. After all, my dad was a dedicated schoolteacher and my mom was a nurse. They even volunteered to join President Kennedy's Peace Corps for a number of years. They were very, very good people, and I received much of my social and moral conscience from them. That is why, when they found out that I wanted to own the corporate ladder *rather than climb* the corporate ladder, they cringed. They thought I had joined *the other side*...and I had. I decided to work out of the B and I side of the Quadrant rather than the E and the S quadrants. I still have the same social and moral conscience they had instilled in me, but they could not see it that way.

To my mom and dad, big business people and investors were the dark side of life. And that is why changing quadrants was more than just a mental change for me. They thought I was rejecting what they had taught us kids...what they thought was good, wholesome, and important. And they thought a good education, a good job, and a nice home were all that I should want in the world. To want to be rich, own companies, invest in businesses throughout the world, and hire people to work for me was joining the dark forces of life. Wanting to be an international businessman and travel the world investing was everything they had taught me not to become. What came to mind for them were pictures of a man who exploited the poor and the working class, and who had lost his religion. So for me, the change felt as if I were leaving and going far away from my family. So although those values seem simple, their roots ran deep throughout my entire being. Years later, my dad realized that changing quadrants did not mean a change in social, moral, or religious values...yet for years he was worried about me. My mom had passed away long before she realized that she had not lost the son she had raised.

It is because our personal core values run deep, that when people ask me, "How do I change quadrants?" I often reply, "Why don't you join a network marketing company?" The main reason I recommend at least looking into a network marketing business is because the change from one side of the quadrant to the other side *is not an over night process.* My rich dad spent years guiding me, teaching me, sometimes scolding me, to become a B and an I. As I stated in Value # 1: The value of life-changing business education, true life-changing education must impact you *mentally, emotionally, physically,* and *spiritually*...and that change may take some time and require some guidance. Some network marketing companies offer that time and guidance.

Why Can't I Do It on My Own?

I am then asked, "Why can't I change from the left side of the Quadrant to the right side on my own?" My answer is, "You can." But for most people, the change is not the easiest of changes. Some of the more famous people who have succeeded in making it big in the B quadrant without joining a network marketing business are Bill Gates; founder of Microsoft; Michael Dell; founder of Dell Computers; Henry Ford; founder of Ford Motor Company; and many others. So it can be done, yet I think in the next few pages you will find out why most people do not make it. They fail to make it on their own not only because of money, but because the price is high when it comes to mental, emotional, physical, and spiritual development.

As I stated in the opening chapter, I succeeded in the B Quadrant without using a network marketing system. That is why I personally know how high the price was...not only in terms of money. When people ask me, "Did you start with nothing?" I reply, "Yes, I started with nothing. I started with nothing 3 times." I say that because I did start with nothing three different times. The first time I started with nothing because I did not have much money when I started my business. The second and third time I started with nothing because my first two major businesses failed. In fact, the second two times I started over, I wished I had started with nothing. *Nothing* would have seemed like heaven. *Nothing* seemed much better than the millions of dollars in debt I was in...debt I accrued because my businesses had failed.

Rebuilding Myself Was More Important Than Making Money

When people say to me that I do not know what it feels like to be poor, I laugh and say, "Do you know what it feels like to lose millions of dollars? Do you know what that much of a loss can do to you mentally, emotionally, physically, and spiritually?" One of the reasons I recommend some network marketing companies is because they do focus on rehabilitating individuals mentally, emotionally, physically, and spiritually. I do know what it feels like to have lost all faith and confidence in myself. And I assure you, losing faith and confidence in myself was worse than losing millions of dollars.

When my first business failed, my poor dad was very upset and embarrassed for me. My rich dad on the other hand said, "Keep going. Most multimillionaires lose three businesses before they get it right." Thankfully it only took me losing two businesses to get it right. But to get it right after failing twice was more a spiritual and emotional challenge and rebuilding process. Once I had rebuilt myself emotionally and spiritually, the money came roaring back.

Rebuilding myself was more important than making money. I recommend some network marketing businesses because they truly do focus on *building,* or *rebuilding* in some cases, the person, and then the person can go on to build his or her own business. If this is of interest to you, your job is to find the network marketing company that has the educational program that focuses first on building you, rather than you, selling the company's plans or products. Once you find the company that is best for you, your job is to do your best to rebuild yourself using their educational plan. All they can do is provide the plan. It is your job to help yourself along that plan. No one can help you if you first do not help yourself.

You can also do it on your own. But please realize that the price of going from the E and S side of the Quadrant to the B and I side of the quadrant can cost you much more than money. For people choosing to use a network marketing system to build a business in the B Quadrant, the price of entry is a lot lower, the risks are lower, and the education and support are there to guide you through this personal development process.

Keep Your Day Job

There are three general types of businesses found in the B

quadrant. They are the big companies that we have all heard of. Companies like Dell Computers or Hewlett Packard, which were started in a dormitory room and a garage. Or you can purchase a franchise such as McDonald's or Taco Bell. The third type of business found in the B quadrant is the network marketing business.

One of the advantages of a network marketing business is the low price of entry. A franchise such as McDonald's will cost at least a million dollars today. So if you have a million dollars or the bank will lend you a million dollars, you may want to jump in and buy a franchise. But if you don't have that kind of money or the time to jump full-time into learning a franchise operation, then a network marketing business may be perfect for you. One big advantage of a network marketing business is that you can remain in the E or S quadrants and start a part-time business in the B quadrant. By doing this, you can take your time getting the education you need without going through the pain, misery, and financial risk I went through gaining my education.

The Power of Mentors

I am often asked, "Will you be my mentor?" I reply as politely as I can and recommend the person look into a network marketing business because of their mentoring programs.

I appreciate more and more the advantage I had by having my rich dad as a mentor. As a schoolteacher, my poor dad did not have the knowledge or experience to teach me what I wanted to know about the B and I quadrants. Without my rich dad, I sincerely doubt if I would have made the journey from the left side of the Quadrant to the right side of the quadrant. The primary role of the mentor in a network marketing company is to guide you from the E and S side of the Quadrant to the B and the I side. And they don't charge you for all the hours they invest in mentoring, coaching, and guiding you. That guidance is priceless.

If you should look into a network marketing company, I strongly recommend looking at the mentors above the person who recommends the business to you. Take the time to meet them and evaluate their sincerity to support you in making the journey from the E and S side to the B and I side. Your mentors in life are important, so choose them wisely.

A Word of Caution

As you may have detected, I have found that *not* all network marketing companies are alike. Just as with anything in life, some are good and some are not so good. Many new network marketing companies fail just as regular businesses fail. Yet the main reason I issue this word of caution is because there are many network marketing companies that mentor you into the S quadrant, not the B quadrant. They do this when they focus only on developing your sales skills and not on the total business skills required to succeed in the B quadrant.

The way you will know they want you in the S quadrant is that they will focus more on product knowledge, sales skills, and how much money you can make. A true B quadrant network marketing company will focus on developing all of you, not just the part of you that can sell and make money for those above you. Doing this may take a little bit more time, and many people quit before they make the complete change. They quit simply because they only wanted to make money rather than change quadrants.

If all you desire is to simply make a few extra dollars, then those types of network marketing companies may be all you need. But for those who want to make the complete change from the left to the right side of the Quadrant, you must look for a network marketing company with training programs that go far beyond just money, product knowledge, and sales ability.

How Long Does It Take to Change Quadrants?

When I am asked, "How long does it take to change quadrants?" I often reply, "I'm still changing." What I mean is that my education never stops in the B and I quadrants. The good news is that the smarter I get in the B and I quadrants, the more money I make and more free time I have.

My recommendation for most people is make up your mind to give the process at least five years. When I say this, I hear many people groan. So if five years seems like forever, then commit for six months. But once you commit, go to everything they recommend you go to. Attend every meeting, all the training sessions, and all the large gatherings you can. The reason I recommend this is because you want to begin to change environments as quickly as possible. Once you change your environment, you begin to change your point of view.

It Starts With a Change of Environments

A change of environments is very important, especially at the start. It is important because people spend most of their time in either the E quadrant or the S quadrant. It is a shame, but people spend most of their waking hours in those quadrants. They spend more time in those quadrants, i.e. at work, than they spend with their families. I suspect that one of the reasons we have so many more problems with young people today is because too many people spend more time at work than they spend with the people they love.

So even though it may mean more time away from your family at first, invest at least six months attending everything you can. I recommend this because there is great truth in the statement that "Birds of a feather flock together."

If you are ready to make the move toward the B and I side, you need to begin to associate as much as possible with people who think the way you want to think.

I remember as a child going between my rich dad's house and my poor dad's house. The two environments were very, very different. Even their parties were different. Today, I have friends who operate from all the different quadrants. But my closest friends, the ones I spend the most time with, are primarily from the B and I quadrants. I have many friends who are in their 40s who are only in the I quadrant because they sold their B businesses and only invest in other businesses today. It is nice to have friends who have money and free time to enjoy life.

Money...But No Free Time

Many of my friends in the E and S quadrants have money, but not much free time. Many make a lot of money, but they cannot afford to stop working. That to me is having money without freedom. That is why it is important to begin to change environments so you can begin to think like people *who have* or *want to have* both money and free time. There is a difference in mindsets, and to find that mindset you need to change environments....quickly I hope.

For many years, my wife and I worked very hard building a business and investing. So at first, it looked as if we worked very hard for very little money and we had very little free time. Today, because of the investment we made, we have money and we have free time. Today we work because we want to...not because we have to...and there is a big difference.

Why Five Years

So if six months is all you can handle right now, make the commitment for six months. I recommend committing to a five year plan for the following reasons.

Reason #1: As stated earlier, learning is a *physical process*...and physical learning sometimes takes longer than just mental learning.

For example, you may decide to learn to ride a bicycle, but the physical learning process may take longer than the mental decision to learn to ride a bicycle. The good news is that once you learn physically, you generally have learned something forever.

Reason #2: On the flip side, *unlearning* is also a physical process. There is a statement that goes, "You can't teach an old dog new tricks." Well, thankfully we are humans and not dogs. Yet, there is some truth to the idea that the older we get, sometimes the harder it is to *unlearn* something we have spent years learning. One of the reasons so many people feel more comfortable in the E and S quadrants is because they feel comfortable and secure there...after all, they spent years learning how to be there. So, many people return there because it is comfortable, even though that comfort is not good for them in the long run.

Take your time to both *unlearn* as well as learn. For some people, the hardest part of switching from the left side of the Quadrant to the right side of the Quadrant is to *unlearn* the point of view of the E and S quadrants. Once you have unlearned what you have learned, I think the change will go much faster and easier.

Reason #3: All caterpillars make a cocoon before becoming butterflies. Flight school was my cocoon. I entered flight school as a college graduate and exited flight school a pilot, ready to go to Vietnam. If I had gone to a civilian flight school, I doubt if I would have been ready for war, even though I was a pilot. What we had to learn as military pilots is different from what civilian pilots have to learn. The skills are different, the intensity of training is different, and the reality of going to war at the end of the training makes things different.

It took me nearly two years to get through basic flight school in Florida. I received my wings, which meant I was a pilot, and was then transferred to advanced flight training at Camp Pendleton, California. There we were trained to *fight* more than to *fly.* I will not bore you with the details, but at Camp Pendleton, the training escalated in intensity.

Now that we had finished flight school and were pilots, we had one year to prepare to go to Vietnam. To prepare, we flew constantly, flying in conditions that tested us mentally, emotionally, physically, and spiritually.

About eight months into the program at Camp Pendleton, something changed inside of me. During one training flight, I finally became a pilot who was ready to go to war. Up to that point in time, I was flying mentally, emotionally, and physically. Some people call it "flying mechanically." On that one training mission, I changed spiritually. The mission was so intense and frightening that suddenly all my doubts and fears were forced out of the way, and my human spirit took over. Flying had become a part of me. I felt at peace and at home inside the aircraft. The aircraft was part of me. I was ready to go to Vietnam.

It was not that I had no fear...for I did. The same fear about going to war was still there. The same fear of dying or, even worse, becoming crippled was still there. The difference was that I was now ready to go to war. My confidence in myself was greater than the fears. And it is this same type of life-changing education I find in many network marketing businesses.

My process of becoming a businessperson and investor has followed much the same process as becoming a pilot ready to go into battle.   It took my failing twice in business before I suddenly found my spirit...a spirit often called the "entrepreneurial spirit." It is a spirit that keeps me on the B and I side, no matter how tough things get. I stay on the B and I side, rather than slipping back to the safety and comfort of the E and S side. I would say it took me 15 years to gain the confidence to feel comfortable in the B quadrant.

I Still Use the Five-Year Plan

When I decide to learn something new, for example, investing in real estate, I still allow myself five years to learn the process. When I wanted to learn how to invest in stocks, I again gave myself five years to learn the process. Many people invest once, lose a few dollars, and then quit. They quit after their first mistake, which is why they fail to learn. My rich dad would say, "A true winner knows that losing is part of the process of winning. It is only the losers of life who think that winners never lose. A loser is someone who dreams of winning and does everything possible to avoid making mistakes."

I still give myself five years to make as many mistakes as possible. I do this because I know that the more mistakes I make and learn from...the smarter I will be in five years. If I make no mistakes for five years, then I am no smarter than I was five years ago. I am only five years older.

The Learning Curve

When people speak of the learning curve, many people picture a graph that may look like this.

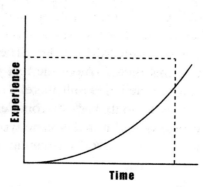

The curving diagonal line that bisects the x and y axis is often referred to as the learning curve.

Nature's Learning Curve

But if you look at nature's learning curve, it is not the learning curve that humans have invented. To see nature's learning curve, all you have to do is watch a young bird get ready to leave the nest for the first time.

The way a young bird leaves the nest and learns to fly is displayed in the following diagram.

This is nature's true learning curve. Many people think that the learning curve of knowledge goes up...and it does. That is the popular idea of the learning curve that humans have invented for themselves.

Yet when you look at nature's learning curve, or what I call the emotional learning curve...that learning curve first goes down, before it heads back up. Many people do not want to feel the emotional down before they feel the exhilaration of flying.

Most people are not successful in life because they are not willing to go through this period of personal doubt and emotional frustration. This happens to many of us because we learn in school that mistakes are bad and should be avoided. So we leave school, sit in the nest, the nest of the E and S quadrant and never learn to fly.

Some of the greatest values of some of the network marketing training systems are that they:

1. Encourage you to leave the nest rather than be a loyal employee,

2. Have a program to support you during the periods of fear, doubt, and frustration,

3. Have mentors who have made the journey themselves, encouraging you to follow after them,

4. Will not fail you as they do in school, or fire you as they do in business, if you make the journey at a pace that is best suited to you, and

5. Want you to make it to the other side.

It's Better Than Going Job to Job

Isn't it better to risk going from the left side of the Quadrant to the right side, without guarantees, than spend your life clinging to job security, or going from job to job, or staying at a job until you are finally too old to work? The value of guiding people across the quadrants is a very important service that many network companies provide.

Value #3: The Value of Access into a 'B' Quadrant Business...

without the high cost of building and maintaining the business.

Someone asked me, "If the B quadrant is so much better than all the other quadrants, then why don't more people start B quadrant businesses?" I was speaking to a church group who asked me to do a class on business and investing.

The answer is not simple...but it can be answered simply, *"Because it is expensive."* Yet, the simplicity of the answer fails to answer the question. When I say it is expensive, the expense of building a B quadrant business goes *far beyond just money*.

One main reason S quadrant businesses remain S quadrant businesses is because the cost of going from the S to the B is far greater than most S quadrant business owners can afford or want to pay. Most S quadrant business people are "hands-on" business people...which means they are actively involved in the business. For the S quadrant businessperson, "letting go" can be a very difficult, if not impossible, thing to do.

How the Rich Get Really Rich

In the third book of the Rich Dad series, *Rich Dad's Guide to Investing*, I share how my rich dad taught me to become really rich. The rich have the ability to take an idea and turn that idea into a B quadrant business. The book goes on to explain how the rich then take the business they build (an asset) and use it to invest in other assets.

In *Rich Dad's Guide to Investing*, I share how you can take your idea and create a multimillion and maybe a multibillion dollar business from that idea. While it is not that hard to do, you will begin to gain some sense as to how expensive building a business can be. And again I measure the word expense in more than mere dollar terms.

A more detailed answer to the question, "Why don't more people build a B quadrant business?" can be found in *Rich Dad's Guide to Investing*. The simple answer is, "It is expensive and it is not easy."

A B Quadrant Business at a Better Price

So Value #3 is that a network marketing business offers all of us the opportunity to access a B quadrant business at a more affordable price and with much less effort. When I began looking into network marketing businesses, I found the same systems my rich dad taught me to build, already created and waiting for anyone who wanted to enter the B quadrant. Most of the network marketing businesses I looked into had already invested the time and the money to build the B quadrant business. All you have to do is invest a few dollars, often less than $500, and instantly, you are in the business.

Once you have joined the business, your job is simply to follow the plan and work at your own speed to build your own B quadrant business. What more could a person ask for? In looking back at the painful and expensive educational path I went through to gain the knowledge, experience, and wisdom of building a B quadrant business, I marvel at how easy the network marketing industry has made it for anyone to enter the B quadrant.

Throughout history, the B quadrant has been the private domain of the rich. In fact, people in the E and S quadrants work for the B quadrant people...yet are never told of the B quadrant. Our school systems educate us to be experts in the E and S quadrants but never educate us as to what it takes to create a B quadrant business. Now the network marketing industry has made access available without having to be rich and without having to go back to get an expensive college education, which only trains you to be a better E or S anyway. The network marketing system and the industry has done a great service by *leveling the playing field.* They did this by making the opportunity for truly great wealth available to anyone willing to follow the system and enter the world of the B quadrant...the quadrant of the ultra-rich.

Success Is Not Measured in Money

During the same talk I mentioned at the start of this chapter, another person asked me, "If the price of entry into the B quadrant is so low with a network marketing business, then why do so few people make it to the top of their system?"

I thanked the person for the question and then added this comment. I replied, "It is not that only a few people make it to the top of a network marketing system. The top of the system is open to everyone, unlike traditional corporate systems, which allow only one person to reach the top of the company." I then went on to explain that I found that the reason most people do not reach the top is simply because they quit too soon, even though the top is wide open.

The person nodded, thought for a while, and then asked, "So if the top is wide open, what reasons did you find for people quitting? Why would someone quit short of the top?"

"Very good question," I replied. I thought for a while and then slowly began my reply. "I know there are many different reasons why people do not make it to the top of a network marketing business. I can only offer what I think and what I have observed."

"And what have you observed?" the young woman asked.

Gathering my thoughts, I began with, "Most people only join to make money. If they do not make money in the first few months or years, they become discouraged, quit, and then often bad-mouth the network marketing industry. Others quit and go looking for a company with a better compensation plan. Joining to make a few quick dollars is not the reason to get into the business."

"If not for money, then why would you tell a person to join?" asked another student in my class.

"Two reasons," I replied. *"Reason number one* is to help yourself and *reason number two* is to help others. If you join for only one of the two reasons, the system *will not* work for you."

"Only one reason isn't enough?" asked another student. "What do you mean by that?" The small class was becoming more interested in the workings of the network marketing industry.

"Sure," I replied. "Reason number one, to help yourself, means that you come to the business primarily to change quadrants. You want to change from the E or the S to the B quadrant."

"Why is that hard to do?" asked a young man. "I have a university degree. Why would the change be hard for me?"

"Another good question," I replied. I went on to explain what I wrote about in Value #1 of this booklet...the value of life-changing business education. I also explained that the change of quadrants required a change mentally, emotionally, physically, and spiritually....and that often took more time than it takes to get a college degree. Explaining further, I went on to say that my rich dad spent over 30 years teaching me to think like a B and I quadrant person and I am still learning to be smarter in those quadrants. "And that is why a network marketing company's educational plan is more important than its products and compensation plan," I ended.

"So what makes the change hard for people?" the same student asked.

"Money," I replied quickly. "Money makes the change difficult."

"What?" another student said out loud. "Why does money make it hard if it does not cost much money to get started?"

"Because true E and S quadrant people do not work unless they work for money. At the core of a true E and S is money."

"And what is at the core of a B or I?" asked the student, now a little angry at me. "You mean to say that they don't work for money?"

"Yes they do, but in a different way," I replied quietly, realizing that I was now striking at some very deep core values. When a person's core values are disturbed, anger is often the byproduct.

"So what does a B or I work hard for?" another student, a middle-aged man, asked.

"A B will build or create an asset...in this case a business system. An I invests in the asset or the system."

"What is the difference?" asked a young woman.

"Sometimes you don't get paid for years and other times you never get paid," I replied quietly. "True E quadrant and S quadrant people will not work for years without getting paid...and they definitely do not like the risk of working hard for years...with the chance of never getting paid. It's not part of their core values. Risk and delayed gratification disturb them emotionally."

"Delayed gratification?" asked the young woman. "I understand the fear involved with risk, but what is the emotion around delayed gratification?"

"Another great question," I replied with a broad smile. "That is one of the most important questions you can ask about emotional intelligence."

"Emotional intelligence?" asked the student who had mentioned his college degree. "Is that different from academic intelligence?"

"Very much so," I replied. "In general, people with high emotional intelligence will often do better than those with high academic intelligence but low emotional intelligence. And that, in part, explains why some people do well in school but do not do well in the real world."

The student with the college degree raised his hand. "So most students leave school and begin looking immediately for a high-paying job in the E quadrant. But someone in the B quadrant will invest even more time in building a B quadrant business...and that person may not get paid for years. That is delaying gratification?"

I nodded my head and said, "Exactly. When I came back from Vietnam, many of my friends and classmates who avoided military service were well into their careers. They were beginning to make pretty good salaries. Instead of following their path, I spent my time with my rich dad, learning to build businesses. I had some financial disasters along the way. Between the years 1975 and 1985 I struggled and often failed. My wife Kim and I were even homeless for about three weeks during this period...but we never went back to the E or S quadrants. Things began picking up by 1986, and by

1994 we were financially free. In 1994, we sold our business and retired. I was 47 and she was 37. We had reached the millionaire status, we had our investments, and we had achieved our goal of financial freedom. My classmates were still working, some still hoping to make $100,000 to $250,000 a year. That is the power of delayed gratification and working hard in the B quadrant. Building a business instead of working at a job and clinging to the illusion of job security. Today we make millions a year and we technically still do not have jobs. We work only at building businesses and investing."

The same person who mentioned his college degree raised his hand and said, "So emotional intelligence coupled with business skills can be an even more powerful education."

I nodded my head and said, "The beauty of network marketing education is that it focuses on developing your emotional intelligence, as well as your business skills."

"You mean work hard for long-term returns rather than short term returns," said another student. "That is what you mean by delayed gratification?"

"That is correct," I replied. "In a recent study of emotional intelligence, it was found that people who could delay gratification often had better and more successful lives than those who could not delay gratification."

"The opposite of delayed gratification is addiction?" asked the young woman.

"That is one example," I said. "People who are addicted have no emotional resistance to certain outside stimuli. People who are addicted to alcohol cannot say "No" to alcohol. Emotionally and physically they crave the substance, even though mentally they may be saying "Don't drink" to themselves. The same is true with cigarettes. You can say to someone who is addicted to cigarettes, "Don't smoke" or "Smoking can kill you and those around you." Mentally, it makes sense, but emotionally and physically they cannot stop. They cannot delay gratification, or have willpower as it is often called, when it comes to their addictions. People without the ability to delay gratification or, are addicted cannot stop when it comes to food, sex, smoking, alcohol, TV, etc. Addiction or lack of ability to delay gratification is a sign of low emotional intelligence."

"And is money an addictive substance?" asked another student.

"Yes…for many people it is. How else can you explain the psychosis around money? People spend their lives working a job they dislike and earning less than they need or want. What a way to waste a life. Others rob people for money. Talk about insane behavior. Others marry for it and others live cheap trying to hoard money. That is truly psychotic behavior in my opinion."

"So that is why you said that money is the main reason people find it difficult in changing from the E or S quadrant to the B quadrant. It is also *money* that causes them to not reach the top of the network marketing system. If they do not see a lot of money in a year or two, they quit, rather than first mentally, emotionally, physically, and spiritually changing quadrants," summarized the young woman. "They want money more than they want to change quadrants."

"Exactly," I replied enthusiastically. "I could not have said it better. Not everyone will agree with me and I don't expect them to, yet that is how I see it."

"So that is why you think the educational systems of a network marketing company are so important. It's the emotional education or emotional intelligence aspect of their programs that you like."

"Very much so," I replied. "As I said, my dad who was a school teacher was literally addicted to job security and a steady paycheck to pay the bills. If that was in any way threatened, he could no longer think straight. His emotions would flare up and he would say things such as, 'Well you have to have money. You have to pay the bills. You can't work and not get paid.'"

"Did he believe in charity?" asked another student.

"Yes, he believed in charity and donating his time. Both my dads were very generous men. But please do not confuse charity and donating of time with building a business and delaying financial rewards. There are differences."

"You're saying your dad was addicted to a paycheck," said another student.

"Yes," I replied. "And that fear of not having money caused my poor dad to have the core value of job security and needing a guaranteed paycheck in the E quadrant rather than investing time in building a business in the B quadrant as my rich dad did."

The college graduate raised his hand and said, "So it is a person's emotions rather than academic training that separates the quadrants. Is that what you are saying?"

"Yes. If you look at the most famous B and I quadrant people in recent history, people such as Henry Ford, founder of Ford Motor Company; Thomas Edison, founder of General Electric; Ted Turner, founder of CNN; Bill Gates, founder of Microsoft; and Michael Dell, founder of Dell Computers, you will note that they are all part of the ultra-rich and they all dropped out of school. Not one of them has a college degree."

"Are you saying to not go to school?" the college graduate challenged.

"No...of course not. A formal education is more important today than ever before. But I am saying that for anyone who dreams of becoming an entrepreneur like Bill Gates or Michael Dell or Anita Roddick of Body Shop fame, many network marketing companies provide the education that traditional schools do not provide. It is the mental, emotional, physical, and spiritual education of the B and I quadrants."

What Is the Cost of Building a B Quadrant Business?

The class for this church group was drawing to a close. I had about a half hour left, so I asked if there were any more questions.

"So what does it cost to build a B quadrant business?" asked another person. "Let's say I don't want to go the network marketing route and I just want to start my own company in the B quadrant. How much would it cost me?"

I thought about his question for a while and said, "At minimum, five years of work and $5 million. That does not count on luck, markets, experience, education, skills, and good timing."

"I have the five years, but I don't have the $5 million. How would I get the money?" asked the participant.

"There are many ways," I said. "But again, that is all part of your B and I quadrant education. Let me point something out to you again."

"What is that?" asked the participant.

"It is the *subject of money* that stops most of you. I can almost hear your mental and emotional minds screaming, "$5 million?" Pausing, I looked around the room and could see the answer in most of their eyes. "Am I correct?" I asked. "It's the money that stops you."

A few nodded. A few glared at me. Finally one brave soul, one of those nodding said, "So you mean the need for money keeps us in the E and S quadrants? And the need of money does not stop you."

I nodded silently. Pausing, I said softly, "And that is why I recommend the network marketing educational system. One of the most important lessons my rich dad taught me was that the lack of money should never stop me from achieving what I wanted to achieve. If you can learn that, you have beaten the addictive power of money, the power that controls most people's lives."

"So even if you had no money, you could find the $5 million to build a business?' "

"I've done it many times. In fact, that is all I do today. But the difference is I was trained by my rich dad to do it. If you want to invest 10 to 20 years of your life and risk millions of dollars learning to do it, then go ahead. Start from scratch. But if you want to keep your daytime job and learn to do it in your spare time, learning with much less risk and expense, then find a network marketing company that will educate you to think like a person in the B and I quadrants."

Will You Be My Mentor?

As I was picking up my notes and leaving the class, a participant raised his hand and said, "Will you give me a job in your company so you can be my mentor?"

I stopped and put my notes down. Doing my best to keep my emotions under control, I paused, looked up at the ceiling and began my reply. The class was deathly silent because they could tell I was not happy with that last question. "I often receive letters from people who write and say, 'I loved your book *Rich Dad Poor Dad.*' They next say something like, 'I have an idea. All you have to do is pay me $1,000 and I will share my idea with you and we can be partners.' Or they write and say something like this person just said which is, 'Please give me a job so I can spend time with you and you can become my mentor.' Why would I not want to pay a partner a $1,000 for his or her idea or be a mentor to someone who needed a job?" I asked the group.

There was a long silence as the group squirmed, thinking about the question I asked them. Finally one brave person raised his hand and asked, "Well what is wrong with paying someone money for their idea?"

"Good question," I said. "First of all, there are plenty of ideas. Everyone I know has a multimillion dollar idea in his or her head. The problem is, most people do not know how to turn that idea into millions of dollars. But why would I not pay this person a $1000 for his or her idea?"

The college graduate raised his hand and said, "Because you don't want to be a partner with them."

"That's correct," I said. "I do not partner with people who need money. People who want to be paid first are generally on the E and S side of the quadrant. I will pay people to be, an E or an S, but not to be my partner on the B and I side."

"That is not fair," another person said out loud. "You should be paid if you contribute something."

"I agree," I said. "But the issue is *when* you get paid. You see a true E and S must be paid. They want their guarantee. A true B and I get paid if and only if the business is built and is successful."

I let them think for a moment. Slowly I began my final remarks. "You see, many people write and say that they love my book *Rich Dad Poor Dad*. But I am afraid many do not get the most important point of the book. And the most important point is found in my rich dad's lesson #1. Who remembers what lesson #1 is?"

Again there was a silence. Finally one participant got out his book and turned to lesson #1. "Lesson #1 of the 6 lessons is 'The rich don't work for money.'"

Nodding, I said, "Do you remember my working for 10 cents an hour? Do you remember my asking for a raise? And do you remember my rich dad's then taking my 10 cents an hour away and telling me to work for free?"

Most of the participants nodded.

"But if you don't work for money, what do you work for?" asked a participant.

"I work to *build* assets, which is what a B quadrant person does, or I work hard to *acquire* assets, which is what a person in the I quadrant does. Once I have my asset, then that asset works hard to give me money...but I will not work just for money. I must have assets. That is why I only work to build or buy assets...assets which in turn make me richer and richer, while working less and less. That is what the rich do, while the poor and middle class work hard for money and then *buy liabilities* instead of *investing in assets*."

"So what kind of asset is a network marketing business?" asked a young woman.

"Oh my goodness," I said out loud. "Thank you for reminding me. I almost forgot to finish what I started to say. Do you remember my saying that there were two reasons required to be successful in a network marketing business?"

The class nodded.

"We have covered reason #1, which is to help yourself. Is that correct?" I asked.

"To help yourself get to the B side of the quadrant. Is that what you mean?" asked a participant.

"That is correct," I said. "And what is reason #2?" I asked.

"To help others," several participants said in unison.

"To help others do what?" I asked.

There was a silence for a moment. "To help others make money?" someone finally ventured.

I smiled and shook my head. "There is that issue of money again. The beauty of most network marketing systems is that you do not really make much money unless you help others leave the E and S quadrant and succeed in the B and I quadrants. If you focus on helping others, then you will be successful in the business. But if you only want to teach yourself to be a B and I quadrant person, then a true network marketing system will not work for you. You may as well go to a traditional business school that focuses only on your becoming a B quadrant person."

"So if I join a network marketing business, my job is to make it to the B and I quadrant and to help others make it also?"

"The system will not work for you unless you have both tasks in mind. The beauty of a network marketing business is that you want to create assets, which are other Bs working under you and their job is then to create other Bs working under them. In traditional business, the focus is for the B to only have Es and Ss working for them," I added.

The college graduate added, "So that means the traditional corporate system is really the pyramid. It is a pyramid because there are a few Bs and Is at the top and more Es and Ss at the base. A network marketing system is a reverse pyramid, which means its primary focus is to bring up more and more Bs to the top."

"Excellent," I replied. "The type of businesses I was taught to build are businesses with me at the top and Es and Ss at the base. I really do not have room at the top for many other Bs. And that is why in my businesses, I strongly recommend all my employees look into network marketing as their own part-time business, while they work in my business full time."

"So why don't you start your own network marketing company?" asked a young man.

"I looked into it, but I finally realized that it was a lot easier to support existing organizations than to create one. I've been trying to tell you that if you really want to take your idea and build your own B quadrant business, then get my book *Rich Dad's Guide to Investing*, and read about what it takes to create a B quadrant business. Then you can decide if you really want to take your multimillion dollar idea and turn it into millions of dollars. You still have that option.

Another participant raised her hand and said, "So one pyramid has its base on the ground and the other pyramid has its base in the air...much like an upside-down pyramid. A pyramid that pulls you up not pushes you down."

"That works for me," I said. "Network marketing businesses give all of us access to what used to be the domain of only the rich. Today, the only question is, "Do you really want to be rich?"

Value #4: The Value of Investing in the Same Investments the Rich Invest In

"Can you tell me how to buy real estate for nothing down?"

I am constantly surprised how many times I am asked questions like this. I know such investments exist, but it puzzled me why so many people were looking for investments that required no money. I found out the reason people are looking for a *nothing-down real estate investment* is because they have nothing to put down.

I am also often asked, "I have $50,000 to invest. What should I invest it in?"

My initial response is, "Is that all you have to invest?" In other words, is this 100% of your investment capital?

And more often than not, the response is, "Yes. This is all I have."

My standard reply to people who have little or no money to invest is, "Interview a few financial planners and create a long-term investment plan." I explain, "Investing is a plan." The first thing a person needs to invest in is a plan, before investing his or her money, and then the person should follow the plan.

Investments for the Rich

In every town, there are rich neighborhoods, middle-class neighborhoods, and poor neighborhoods. This is true throughout the world. The same is true with investments.

I recommend people look into network marketing because of the investment advantages the business offers. Successful people in the network marketing business can afford to invest in the same investments the very rich invest in. Most people in the E and S quadrants cannot afford to invest in the investments of the rich simply because they don't make enough money.

In America, the Securities and Exchange Commission, the SEC, requires that a person have an annual salary of at least $200,000 a year for an individual or $300,000 per annum for a couple, and over $1,000,000 in net worth. This is a minimum requirement to be considered an accredited investor and to qualify for the investments of the rich. Less than 4% of all Americans meet this requirement. This means that only a few people are allowed to invest in the most profitable investments in the world....one more reason the rich get richer.

Two Reasons for Investing

In the third book of the Rich Dad series, *Rich Dad's Guide to Investing*, I cover the two basic types of money problems...the problem of not enough money and the problem of *too much* money. It follows then that there are also two primary reasons for investing. They are:

1. People invest because they *don't have enough money.*
2. People invest because they have *too much money.*

Years ago, my rich dad began talking to me about these two basic types of money problems. He said, "Everyone has money problems...even the rich. The poor have the problem of not enough money, and the rich have the problem of too much money. Which type of money problem do you want when you grow up?" Needless to say, I made plans to have the problem of too much money.

My rich dad also said, "People raised in a family with the problem of not having enough money often think that *not having* enough money is the only kind of money problem there is."

One of the advantages I had by having both a rich dad and a poor dad is that I could see the two types of money problems. My poor dad often said, "I wish I had money to invest, but I don't make enough money." My rich dad often said, "I need to find more investments because I am making too much money. If I don't invest my excess money, the government will take it from me in taxes."

Investing Because You Have Too Much Money

A few months ago, I was teaching investing to a network marketing company's leaders and their families. There were about 200 in the class. The leaders of the business invited me to teach the group how to invest because many of them had the problem of *too much* money and the problem was, instead of investing their excess money, they were simply wasting it. As one of the leaders said to me, "We do a good job of teaching them to be successful business owners in the B quadrant, but we do not teach them what to do with their money in the I quadrant."

Once the group understood the power that comes from harnessing the advantages of both the B quadrant and the I quadrant, a whole new world of financial possibilities opened up to them. For many of them, the lights went on and they could finally see the magic kingdom of money.

The morning session of the class was simple enough with my usual big picture lecture on the different investment strategies. I then had them play my educational board game CASHFLOW 101. Several were already experts with 101 and so they went on to play CASHFLOW 202, the advanced investor game.

After the game was over, I spent an hour debriefing the players, finding out what they had learned. The conversation was lively and animated. Some of the comments were:

1. "I saw my whole financial life flash in front of me. I make money and then I spend it all. I now know I can stop that poor man's way of managing my money. I finally learned how to manage my money like a rich person."

2. "I realize I need a new accountant. Mine may be a good accountant, but he is not a good investor."

3. "It was a tough game...but it was real life. I want to change the way I run my real life. It does not make sense to make money and then blow it. I'm going to treat the money I earn with more respect."

4. "I'm happy because something has finally taught me how to have money work hard for me, instead of me working hard for money. This game has changed my life."

5. "The game was good because I could see my past, my present, and my future...and my future is going to be very different from my past and present."

In the afternoon session, we went into more strategic planning. Pointing to the B and I quadrants of the Cashflow Quadrant I said, "We are now going to talk about how to harness the power of these

two quadrants."

One of the participants raised his hand and said, "You mean there are different investment strategies for the different Quadrants?"

"Definitely," I said. " Years ago, my rich dad drew the Quadrant and then drew arrows as I am doing now."

"What does that diagram represent?" the same participant asked.

"It simply represents the way the different quadrants invest. People from the E, or employee, quadrant will often want safe, secure investments, just as they value a safe, secure job with a good pension plan. If they do invest on their own, many will invest in mutual funds. These people will often use such words as "diversify, invest for the long term, and dollar cost averaging." If they want a little bit more excitement, they go to a casino or buy a few lottery tickets…but for the most part, their investments are safe and secure, or at least they hope they are."

"And the S quadrant invests differently?" asked another participant.

"A true S quadrant investor, someone who is self-employed or a small business owner will invest in what I call the 'hands-on' method of investing. Being the rugged individuals of the work world, they invest like the rugged individuals they are. So if they invest in real estate, they often invest in fixer-uppers…because they want to be hands-on. They often like to renovate things. They will also manage the real estate and sell the real estate on their own, just to save the fees and commissions. If a toilet breaks, they fix it. Rarely will this investor go beyond a duplex (two units) or a four-plex (four rental units). Anything more than 50 units would probably be too big an investment and too hard to be completely hands-on, especially when it comes to fixing toilets. If they invest in stocks, these do-it-yourselfers like to day-trade with stock options, or they like to read the financial papers, watch the investor news on television, and pick their own stocks," I said.

"So what is the difference in the way the B quadrant business owner invests and the way the S quadrant business owner invests?" another participant asked. "I ask because what you just said upset me."

"What did I say that upset you?" I asked.

"Because I'm that guy who owns a duplex. I'm the guy who fixes those toilets. And I'm the guy who tries to pick stocks by reading the financial newspapers and watching the financial television networks. What you just said is that I'm in the B quadrant, but I am still investing like an S."

Investing Like the Ultra-Rich

"Could be," I said, laughing. "At least you're active and investing and there is nothing wrong with investing like an S quadrant person. But I am here today to tell you that you have the potential to invest the way the ultra-rich invest...just because you have the courage to work in the B quadrant.'

"You mean I'm wasting my time investing the way I am," commented the person who admitted to being an S quadrant investor.

"I would not say you're wasting your time...because after all you are gaining experience, but I would say that you are not focusing on harnessing the potential you have."

"What do you mean by harnessing the potential we have?" asked a woman about my age sitting at the back of the room.

"Most of the self-made ultra-rich of the world made their money by harnessing the power of both the B and the I quadrants."

"You mean there are people who are in only the B quadrant and people only in the I quadrant?" the same woman asked.

"Sure," I said. "Just as there are E and S quadrant people who are only in one quadrant. In fact, many people in the network marketing business are really only in one quadrant...which is why I was brought in. I was brought in to teach you how to harness the power of both quadrants."

"You mean we're not maximizing the potential of what we have?" asked the woman.

"Exactly. If more people truly understood the potential power of your network marketing business and the I quadrant, more people would get into the business. Marrying the power of the B quadrant and the I quadrant gives you the same power the ultra-rich have...in fact that is what made most of them ultra-rich. You talk about building a business when you could also be teaching people how they can become rich or ultra-rich."

"And what do you mean by ultra-rich?" a participant asked.

"Some people who make $150,000 a year and have a $5 million portfolio or retirement package, may think of themselves as rich. But according to *Forbes Magazine*, the definition of rich is $1 million or more in annual income, preferably without working. My rich dad's definition of ultra-rich was someone who makes at least $1 million a month. He did not quite make that category of rich, but he was very close. I have reached Forbes's definition of rich and I am now working on becoming ultra-rich. You all have the potential to become ultra-rich if you harness the financial power of both the B and I quadrants. That is why *Rich Dad's Guide to Investing* was really written for you. Most E and S quadrant investors do not have that much power."

The room sat quietly. After a few moments a handsome young man raised his hand and asked, "Do you mean we are not saying the right things to the right people?"

I nodded and said, "I often see people who come to the business because they need a job or need money...and your organization does a great job of lifting their spirits, giving them hope, and teaching them to build their own business. And that is a very important service your organization provides. But you are often not talking to the person who is already financially successful but has hit a dead end in their earning power. Someone may already be making $150,000 to $250,000 but realizes he or she has hit his or her earning ceiling. Many S quadrant people fall into this category.

They cannot earn much more simply because they lack the leverage a B quadrant business offers."

"We do talk to a lot of people like that and a few do come in," a participant chimed in a little defensively.

"I know you do and I do not mean to offend you or your efforts. But I can tell you that when I was approached to join this business, nothing said to me really interested me. I was already building a successful business and on my way to becoming a millionaire. If I had been told I could help other people by giving them a hand-up instead of a hand-out, I might have been more interested. By helping others succeed, you have the ability to become ultra-rich in this business."

Again, there was a silence. Finally a brave soul raised her hand and said, "You mean being a millionaire is not a big deal?"

I replied, "I think you could say it that way." I continued. "Being a millionaire is good, but it is not that uncommon today. Many professional athletes, such as football players, are millionaires. Today there are many ways to become a millionaire, but only a few ways to become ultra-rich...and you have that potential."

"So what are we missing?" asked the young woman who had asked the previous question.

"Your system has the potential power to make people ultra-rich...like Michael Dell." Again I held up my book, *Rich Dad's Guide to Investing;* pointing to it I said, "I wrote this book for people like you...people who have the drive to become rich...and maybe ultra-rich. But you have to think that such wealth is possible for you...and the way it is possible is by utilizing both quadrants."

"We have to think that that much wealth is possible?" asked a young woman.

Nodding, I said, "If you don't think it's possible, then you close your mind and it is not possible."

"And how do we begin to think it's possible?" the same young woman asked.

"By educating yourself. Start with this book and know that everything in this book is possible for you...if you study and dedicate yourself. Some people reading this book may be disappointed because attaining the status of the ultra-rich is not possible for them. Very few E and S quadrant people have access to the financial horsepower you have."

"Why is that?" asked a participant.

The Power of Leverage

"I said it before and I will say it again. In most cases, the people in E and S quadrants lack one of the most important words in business...and that word is *leverage*."

"What do you mean by *leverage?*"

"*Leverage* is one of those words that can mean many different things. What I mean is that you have the power to earn more and more by working less and less. A person in the E and S quadrant, in most cases, must work more and more if they want to earn more. The problem is, the people in the E and S quadrant are marketing a finite commodity, their time. There are only so many hours in a day...so the E and S can earn only so much in a day."

"We do say that to people, so what are *you* saying that we *aren't* saying?" asked the handsome young man.

"Three of you have tried to get me into your business," I replied. "I let the three of you tell me why I should join your business and you did a very good job. All you talked to me about was *building the business* and making a lot of money."

"So what is wrong with that?" asked the young man. "That is what we do. That is what you do. Isn't it?"

"Yes, I build businesses...but I don't really build a business for money's sake. The business is an asset. Building a business is hard work, and I don't like hard work. I was born and raised in Hawaii. I am basically lazy and I love my free time. I'd rather be sitting on the beach or surfing. That sounds like fun to me. That is why I work hard at building a business. I refuse to work in the E and S quadrants...because I am lazy."

"I'm missing something," the young man said, wondering if I was pulling his leg. "You're lazy, so you work hard to build businesses. That doesn't make sense."

"It makes sense if you realize that I am not really a businessman. I am really an investor, and I enjoy the lifestyle that my investments allow me to have."

"So once the business is up and running, you are free to invest in real estate, stocks, bonds, and other businesses," the young man said quietly. "Building a business gives you the two main ingredients an investor needs, time and money."

"Lots of time and lots of money," I said quietly. "And I do not waste my time investing in a duplex and fixing toilets, or trying to pick stocks. Those are investments for the S quadrant, which can also mean small investor. And most small investors are trying to invest to make money. They're trying to invest because they don't have enough money. I invest from the B quadrant because I have too much money. Because I have too much money, the government in some ways forces me to invest my money or lose it to taxes. People in the E quadrant don't have any choice. The government taxes their earnings before they get paid, giving them very little choice about investing. Since I have a lot of money and I have a chance to invest it before being taxed, I invest in big properties, big stock plays, and in other businesses. I build a business so that I can have the money to invest in the investments only the rich invest in...and that is how you become ultra-rich."

"You only invest in building a B quadrant business because you want the money to invest. Is that what I hear you saying?"

"Not exactly. On the surface it looks that way, but let me try to explain something a little bit more complicated to you." I then drew the diagram of the Cashflow Quadrant and said,

"Do you remember the story about my rich dad, explaining this diagram to me when I was a little boy?"

The class nodded.

"And who remembers the importance of the dates 1943, 1986, and 1215?"

"1215 was the signing of the Magna Carta," a young woman volunteered. "That was the year the rich took the power away from King John of England. From then on, the rich made the rules."

"Very good," I said. "So given the choice, I want to invest from the B side because the business owners have the best rules for investing, simply because they make the rules. Continue."

"America was founded by a tax revolt, which began in 1773, with the Boston Tea Party. America grew rapidly because it was a tax-free nation. In 1943, the law changed and all employees in America had taxes taken from their paychecks. In other words, the government got paid before they got paid."

"You've learned well," I remarked, amazed that anyone would remember my talk on the history of taxes. "Paying taxes was said to be a patriotic duty because World War II was on...but it was the worker in the E quadrant who paid most of the taxes. The people in the S and the B quadrants still had control over how much they paid, and when they paid their taxes."

Continuing, the young lady said, "In 1986, the tax law changed and it negatively affected people primarily in the S quadrant, more specifically the doctors, attorneys, engineers, architects, accountants, and other professional people. It seems that again, the rich had changed the rules to favor their quadrant. The rich make more money but pay less in tax simply because they operate out of the B quadrant," said the young woman.

The B Quadrant Advantage Is in the I Quadrant

"Thanks for paying attention," I said. "I could not have said it better. That is why I build businesses in the B quadrant not the S quadrant. But the main point is that just being in the B quadrant alone is not enough. It does not give you the full power of the B quadrant."

"The B quadrant is not enough?" a participant repeated in a confused tone.

"No," I replied. "There are many people who build businesses in the B quadrant, but not all of them use the power of the B quadrant."

"Why is that?" asked the same participant.

"Because the true power of the B quadrant is not found in the B quadrant, it is found in the I quadrant," I said.

The class sat quietly until someone finally asked, "Can you explain what you mean?"

"I could," I said, "but that discussion is far beyond the time I have today. For now, just remember that the tax laws favor the B quadrant via the I quadrant.

The class sat quietly. A few were getting excited while others were kind of puzzled. I would say that many did not want to go beyond a B quadrant business. A participant raised her hand and confirmed what I was thinking. She said, "But what if all I want to do is build a business. Do I have to invest after that?"

"No," I said. " I realize that this may be overloading you today. But when you begin to have the kind of extra money that the rich have, you will be glad you chose the B quadrant to work hard in."

"You mean when we have the problem of having too much money?" asked another participant.

"Yes. When you have the problem of having too much money, you will be glad you chose to build a B quadrant business. When the government starts coming after you to pay more and more in taxes, at least you will have ways to *legally* invest your money instead of paying it in taxes. And if you do pay taxes, you will pay at a lower tax rate, legally." Turning to the flip chart, I drew the following diagram. "This is the loophole that gives the rich the advantage."

Employee

Income	
Expense	
Taxes	

Asset	Liability

Business

Income	
Expense	
	Taxes

Asset	Liability

Turing back to the group, I said, "The difference between the financial statement of the employee and the financial statement of the business owner is staggering. If you recall from *Rich Dad Poor Dad*, Rich Dad's lesson #2 is the importance of financial literacy. I suspect one reason they don't teach financial literacy in school is because our schools train people to be employees. If employees could read a financial statement, they would know why the owners of the company get richer and richer, while the employees work harder and harder, only to pay more and more in taxes. Taxes are employees' single largest expense."

A young woman raised her hand and said, "You mean the employee gets taxed first and a business owner gets taxed last. That is the loophole you talk about?"

"It's one of them," I replied. "And there are many more."

"But that is not fair," she said.

"I agree," I said. "And as I said, there are many more advantages the B quadrant has, but you must know the tax laws, corporate laws, insurance laws, and investment laws."

"So you are saying that it works best with the combination of both the B and I quadrant?"

"Yes, in most cases," I replied. "I am not a tax attorney or accountant, but in principle, that is what I am saying."

"So if we waste our money on silly things and do not

understand investing, we do not harness the power of the B and the I quadrant?" asked another participant.

Nodding, I said, "Yes...that is what I am saying." Holding up the game board from *CASHFLOW*, I pointed to the first and then to

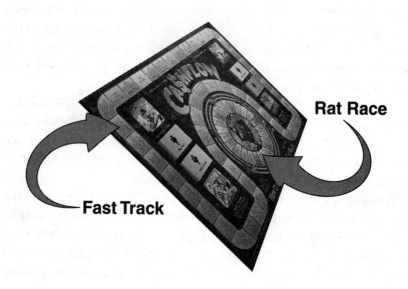

the second track on the board."

"Pointing to the Rat Race I said, "95% of all people are trapped in the Rat Race." Then pointing to the Fast Track I said, "And the Fast Track represents the investments of the rich."

The class looked at the game board with a new interest. "So this game is real life, isn't it?" a participant asked.

Nodding, I said, "I designed the game to teach as many things as possible. Things like accounting, cash flow management, investing, investing vocabulary, how to think strategically, and more. But I also wanted people to know that there were two worlds of investing...one for the rich and one for the masses trapped in the Rat Race of life. Very few people have the opportunity to invest as the rich do...investing in investments found only on the Fast Track. All of you in this room have that opportunity...but first you must build your businesses and teach others to build their businesses."

"Is building a business the only way to invest on the Fast Track?"

asked a participant.

"No it isn't," I replied. "As I said earlier, if you are a professional athlete making millions of dollars a year, or the movie star, or rock star, or CEO of a major corporation, or a doctor making millions of dollars, you will be granted access to the real Fast Track. Many people get to the Fast Track through the I quadrant, by being professional investors. Yet, the way most of the ultra-rich get to the real Fast Track is through building a business...in most cases, a B quadrant business. Very few E and S quadrant people will ever enter the real Fast Track of life."

There was another long silence in the room. I could tell that what I had been saying was sinking in. Finally a participant said, "So if we build our business and then begin to invest in the investments on the Fast Track, we can join the ranks of the ultra-rich?"

"Yes." Pausing for a while, I then added, "but you have to know that it is possible for you. That is why you need to understand both the B and the I quadrants."

A participant raised his hand and said, "So to invest a lot of time doing the small investment deals found in the Rat Race is a waste of time?"

"For people like you who are working to build a business in the B quadrant it might be," I said. "Why would you spend your time with small investments when you could focus on building your business and then jump straight to the Fast Track?"

"But isn't the investing experience gained from the Rat Race important?" a young man asked.

"Yes it is important...very, very important. But what I see happening in the real world is that many E quadrant and S quadrant people are trying to escape the Rat Race via the I quadrant. These individuals are buying mutual funds, picking stocks, day trading, and buying small duplexes. For many of them, it is a good plan. But you are different. You have the power of a B quadrant business...a business that has virtually no earning limitations and no international boundaries. Learn to do small deals so you have experience doing big deals. But don't waste your time trying to escape the Rat Race by investing in investments of the masses. Build your business and invest in the investments of the rich...the people who invest because they have the problem of too much money. Don't invest like people who don't have enough money....because they don't have much money, they hope to make money from their investments. Those people never get the best investments. The best investments only go to those who have too much money."

Again there was a silence in the room. A participant said, "So trying to get out of the Rat Race via our small investments isn't that good an idea?"

"Good question," I replied. "Let me ask those of you who have played *CASHFLOW 101* this question. 'In real life, does a person getting out of the Rat Race automatically qualify to get on to the Fast Track?'"

The group thought for a while. Finally a young woman said, "No. There are many people who get out of the Rat Race. In theory a person who has a retirement plan is out of the Rat Race. But in real life, didn't you say that very few people actually qualify for the investments of the Fast Track, even if they are out of the Rat Race?

Before I could answer the question an older gentleman raised his hand and said, "I can tell you that working all your life to retire on a small pension does not make much sense. Do you know how much my company's pension is? It is hardly enough to survive on. Many of my friends have retired with so little money that all they retire to is a slower and poorer Rat Race."

Nodding, I said quietly, "This is why I come to speak to you. All of you have the potential to live very different lives because you chose to invest your time in building a B quadrant business. Most people will work hard all their lives only to wind up out of time and out of money. That is a tragedy."

How to Become Ultra-Rich

A participant raised his hand and said, "But you said that we had the potential to become ultra-rich. We could become richer than many movie stars, rock stars, athletic stars, even the president of the company I work for today."

"That is correct," I said. "Far beyond what your boss is making."

"That is what I am interested in," said the same participant. "How do we take this business and become ultra-rich."

"First of all you have to think it is possible," I said.

"Don't most people think it is possible?" asked another participant.

"I think most people think it is possible, but not for them. They think that someone else can do it but not them. You see, unless you think it is possible for you, it is impossible," I replied softly. "Most people dream of someday becoming a millionaire, but very few people have the potential of making a million dollars a month and more. That reality is just not in their reality."

"Is it in your reality?" asked a participant.

"Of course," I replied.

"And how did you get that reality?"

"My rich dad put it there," I said. Pausing for a moment, I then asked, "What reality about money did your parents put in your head?"

"Not a million dollars a month," said a young man. "My mom and dad thought a job that paid $100,000 a year meant you were rich."

"Most people do," I said.

"So how do we get that reality in our head...the reality of earning a million dollars a month or more?" asked the same young man.

"You have to put it there," I said. "No one else can do that for you."

"Why do you say that?" a young woman asked.

"I say that because I can see it in your eyes. I can tell that most of you don't really want that reality because it is outside of your reality. Like most of you, I came from a family that was not rich. My mom and dad often said words such as, 'I can't afford it.' Or 'Do you think money grows on trees?' Or 'Money does not make you happy.' Or 'Rich people aren't happy.' In my family the reality was the reality of *not enough money*. In order for me to escape the reality of my family, I had to look for ideas outside of that reality...and that is what my rich dad did for me. In fact, that is all he did for me. He gave me the reality and taught me how to make the reality real."

"And can you give that reality to us?" the older gentleman asked.

"I already have given you that reality," I said. "The question is, now do you want to make it your reality?"

The older gentleman smiled and said, "I understand what you are getting at. You are saying that right now some of us are already *rejecting* the idea and some of us want to accept the idea...the idea of becoming ultra-rich."

I nodded. "Most people reject it," I said. "Most people find a reason why the idea is unrealistic. Some people attack me, saying that I give people unreal expectations or false hope. But I can never give anyone unreal expectations or false hope. If you notice, I am only sharing with you my expectations and my hopes. It is up to you to determine if they are real or false for you."

"But you have not made the ultra-rich category?" asked the older man. "Yet you say you are going for it."

"That is correct," I said. "Right now I am just rich. My goal is to someday be ultra-rich. The point is, I have not given up on the goal, a goal I made over 25 years ago, and I take a step in that direction each and every day."

"So how do you know you can make it?" asked a young man.

"I don't know if I can make it...in fact it took me longer because I failed twice along the way...but I am still going for it," I said. "What I do know is that other people have made it. People like Bill Gates and Michael Dell. And they made it in their thirties...or maybe earlier."

"And you are saying we have that potential?" a young woman asked.

"Yes. I have met many people in network marketing who have made it to the ultra-rich category. I know because I have seen the investments they have invested in through their business. I have seen the giant office buildings that they own, not rent; their shopping malls; companies they are major shareholders in; large residential subdivisions; ranches; and more. They could never have bought these investments as an E or S, but they could with their B quadrant business; a business without earnings limitations can afford the investments of the rich. So you are on the right path. You have the potential if you work at building your business, continue to study, learn about investments on the Fast Track, and keep improving yourself from the inside out. But only you can do that for yourself...and there are no guarantees."

"So how do we study about investments on the Fast Track of your *CASHFLOW* Game?" asked a young woman.

"I wrote about those investments in *Rich Dad's Guide to Investing*. As I said, many Es and Ss read that book and become disappointed. But all of you have the power to invest in the investments of the rich. Investments that by law require you to be a millionaire before you can invest."

"What do you suggest we do?" asked the older gentleman. "I'm running out of time. What if I don't have enough time? Can I still make it?"

"First of all, stop using age as an excuse. Just remember Colonel Sanders did not start Kentucky Fried Chicken until he was in his late 60s. My rich dad always said, 'Losers use their life's situations as excuses to fail, and winners use their life's situations as their reasons to succeed.' The Colonel used his age as his reason to succeed, and he went into the ultra-rich category at an age when most people had retired."

"Point well taken," the older gentleman said. "So what do you suggest?"

"First of all, I suggest all of you read *Rich Dad's Guide to Investing* so you get an overall idea of the world of investing. Then if you want to make becoming ultra-rich a part of your reality, I suggest you get together in groups and study a chapter at a time, starting with Chapter 20, which is the chapter on the 90/10 riddle. Take your time. Ask people to read the chapter before coming to a meeting, and then get together and discuss each chapter in depth. Take your time. You will find that via this method of group study and discussion, you will expand your minds beyond your current realities on investing."

"You mean most of us only think about investments for the poor and middle class?" asked the older gentleman. "So we need to educate ourselves on the investments that the rich invest in. We need to make the investments of the rich a part of our reality."

"Exactly," I said. "That is what my rich dad gave me. He gave me a reality on the world of investments that only the rich know about. Once I had that reality, I knew my life's path, which I am still on."

"So most of us only know about mutual funds, stock picking,

investing in small real estate deals because that is our reality on the world of investing. Is that what you are saying?"

"That is exactly what I am saying," I responded. "Most people think about investing from the E and S quadrants. They think investing is risky, and they want to play it safe. They invest in safe, pre-packaged investments, just the way they buy meat at the grocery store. The rich invest in the ranch that pre-packages the investments that the poor and middle class buy. It is a completely different reality."

"So start with chapter 20 and expand our reality. Then get together regularly and study the rest of the chapters beyond chapter 20. You think that exercise will open our minds to better understand the investments of the rich...which you are saying are available to us."

I nodded. "If you understand how much fun and how exciting investments on the Fast Track are, you will wonder why so many people look primarily for safe, pre-packaged, small investments. At least I do," I replied. "But I guess that is what happens when you only know of investments inside your reality. I also think that once you understand how powerful the investments of the rich are, you will want to build your B quadrant business even faster...because as I said, the fun of life is investing your money and having your money work hard for you."

"Is there another step you recommend for me?" asked the older gentleman.

"Yes," I said. "Step 2 is a very important step. I suggest you use all these young people and not-so-young people around you as energy and support to push you forward. Once you have the new reality, use their support to make your new reality. Ask for their help. They want to help you make it. But they can't help you unless you want to help yourself and then allow them to help you."

The older gentleman sat quietly. I could see that asking for support was not comfortable for him. I know because men are often trained to think that asking for support is a sign of weakness. I know it is true for many women also. Realizing that he was uncomfortable about asking for support, I asked him to stand and look around the room.

The older gentleman hesitated, and then finally began to stand.

I could tell he was not comfortable with my request. After reaching his full height, he slowly lifted his eyes and he gazed out on the several hundred people in the room. Everyone was looking back at him and smiling. Their eyes were saying that they were there for him.

I then asked, "How many of you here are willing to support him?"

There was a loud rush of air as hands shot up, high into the air, wanting to be seen. The older gentleman looked around the room. All around him were arms up in the air, attached to eyes filled with love and support. Suddenly his emotions came boiling up from inside him. His eyes began to tear as he looked back at the sea of support that surrounded him. In silence, he held his gaze, meeting many people eye to eye, soul to soul. He then nodded his head, and quietly said, "thank you." Trembling a little, he took his seat as the room spontaneously broke into loud enthusiastic applause.

Once the applause died down, I picked up my books and said, "The beauty of this business is that all you have to do to succeed is to help other people get the same things you want. This business is not measured in how much money you make, but in how many people you help and how many lives you change." I thanked them and left the room.

NETWORK 6

Value #5: The Value of Living Your Dreams

"Many people don't have dreams," my rich dad said.

"Why?" I asked.

"Because dreams cost money," he said.

Rekindling the Dream

My wife Kim and I went to a gathering where a top producer in a network marketing company was showing off his 17,000-square foot mansion, with an eight car garage, as well as the eight cars to fill it, his limousine, and all his other toys. The house and toys were impressive, but the thing that really impressed me was that the city had named the street his house was on, after him. When I asked him how he got the city to do that, he said, "Easy, I donated money to build a new elementary school and a library. When I did that, the city allowed me to name the street after my family." At that point, I realized that his dream was far bigger than my dream. I have never dreamed of having a street named after me or donating enough money to build a school and a library. Leaving his home that night, I realized that it was time for me to increase the size of my dreams.

One of the more important values I have found in good network marketing businesses is that they stress the importance of going for and living your dreams. The top producer we were visiting was not showing off his material goods merely to show off. He and his wife were speaking to the group about the lifestyle they had achieved in order to inspire the group to live their dreams. It was not about the big house or the toys or how much they cost. It was about inspiring others to go for their dreams.

Killing the Dream

In *Rich Dad Poor Dad*, I wrote about my poor dad constantly saying, "I can't afford it." I also wrote that my rich dad forbade his son and me from saying those words. Instead, he required us to say, "How can I afford it?" As simple as those statements are, the difference between them was very important to my rich dad. He said, "Asking yourself 'How can I afford things' allows you to have bigger and bigger dreams."

Rich dad also said, "Be aware of people who want to kill your dreams. There is nothing worse than a friend or loved one killing your dreams. There are people who may innocently or not so innocently, say things such as:

1. "You can't do that."
2. "That is too risky. Do you know how many people fail?"
3. "Don't be silly. Where do you come up with such ideas?"
4. "If it is such a good idea, why hasn't someone else done it before?"
5. "Oh I tried that years ago. Let me tell you why it won't work."

I have noticed that people who kill other people's dreams are people who have given up on their own dreams. When you look at the educational pyramid mentioned earlier, dreams often come from the spiritual side of learning, and people who kill dreams tend to come from the emotional side of the pyramid.

Why Dreams Are Important

My rich dad explained the importance of dreams in this way, "Being rich and being able to afford a big house are not important. What is important is striving, learning, doing your best to develop your personal power to afford the big house. It is who you become in the process of affording the big house that is important. People who dream small dreams continue to live lives as small people."

As my rich dad said, it was not the home that was important.

My wife Kim and I have owned two very large homes…and I agree that it was not the size of the house or becoming rich that was important. It was the size of the dream that was important. When my wife and I were broke, we set a goal that when we had made over a million dollars we would buy a big house. When our business grossed over a million dollars, we bought our first big house and then sold it soon after. We sold it because we had moved on to achieving a new dream. In other words, the house and earning a million dollars was not the dream. The house and money were the symbols of becoming people who could achieve our dreams. Today, we again own a big home, and again the home is just the symbol of the dream we achieved. Our big house is not the dream; it is who we had to become in the process that is the dream.

Rich Dad said it this way, "Big people have big dreams, and small people have small dreams. If you want to change who you are, begin by changing the size of your dream." When I was broke and lost most of my money, my rich dad said, "Never let this temporary financial setback diminish the size of your dream. It is the vision of your dream that will pull you through this rough period of life." He also said, "Broke is temporary, and poor is eternal. Even if you are broke, it does not cost you anything to dream of being rich. Many poor people are poor because they have given up on dreaming."

Different Types of Dreamers

When I was in high school, my rich dad explained that there were five kinds of dreamers. They are:

1. ***Dreamers who dream in the past.*** Rich Dad said there are many people whose greatest achievements in life are behind them. Al Bundy of TV's sitcom *Married With Children* is a classic example of someone whose dreams are behind him. For those who may not be familiar with the show, Al Bundy is a grown man who still re-lives his days in high school, when he was a football star who scored four touchdowns in one game. That is an example of someone who continues to dream in the past.

Rich Dad would say, "A person who dreams in the past is a

person whose life is over. That person needs to create a dream in the future, in order to come back to life."

It is not only ex-football stars that live in the past. Other examples of people who still live in the past are people who still revel in getting good grades, being prom king or queen, graduating from a prestigious university, or being in the military. In other words, their best days are behind them.

2. ***Dreamers who dream only small dreams.*** Rich Dad said, "These types of dreamers will dream only small dreams because they want to feel confident they can achieve them. The problem is, even though they know they can achieve them, they never do achieve them."

This type of dreamer did not make much sense to me until one day I asked this man, "If you had all the money in the world, where would you travel?"

His reply was, "I would fly to California to visit my sister. I haven't seen her in 14 years, and I would love to see her. Especially before her children get any older. That would be my dream vacation."

I then said, "But that would only cost you about $500 dollars. Why don't you do that today?"

"Oh I will, but not today. I'm just too busy right now."

After meeting this individual, I realized that this type of dreamer is more common than I thought. These people live their lives having dreams they know they can achieve, but they never seem to get around to living their dreams. Later in life you can hear them say, "You know, I should have done that years ago, but I just never got around to doing it."

My rich dad said, "These type's of dreamers are often the most dangerous. They live like turtles, tucked away in their own quiet padded room. If you knock on the shell and peak in one of the openings, they often lunge out and bite you." The lesson is let dreaming turtles dream. Most aren't going anywhere, and that is perfectly fine with them.

3. ***Dreamers who have achieved their dreams and have***

not set a new dream. A friend of mine once said to me, "Twenty years ago, I dreamed of becoming a doctor. I became a doctor and now I am just bored with life. I enjoy being a doctor, but something is missing."

This is an example of someone who has successfully achieved his dream and continues to live in the dream. Boredom usually is a sign that it is time for a new dream. My rich dad would say, "Many people are in professions they dreamed of in high school. The problem is they have been out of high school for years. It is time for a new dream and a new adventure."

4. *Dreamers who dream big dreams but do not have a plan on how to achieve them...* so they wind up achieving nothing. I think we all know someone in this category. These are people who say, "I've just had a major break, through. Let me tell you about my new plan." Or, "This time things will be different." Or "I'm turning over a new leaf." Or "I'm going to work harder, pay off my bills, and invest." Or "I just heard of a new company coming to town, and they are looking for someone with my qualifications. This could be my big break."

My rich dad said, "Very few people achieve their dreams on their own. People like this often try to achieve a lot, but they try and do it on their own. People like this should keep dreaming big, find a plan, and find a team that will help them make their dreams come true."

5. *Dreamers who dream big dreams, achieve those dreams, and go on to dream bigger dreams.* I think that most of us would like to be this kind of person. I know I would.

One of the most refreshing things that happened to me while looking into some of the network marketing businesses was that I found myself dreaming even bigger dreams. The business encourages people to dream big dreams and achieve their big dreams. Many traditional businesses don't want people to dream personal dreams. Too many times I meet people who have friends or work for businesses that actively kill a person's dreams. I support the network marketing industry because it is an industry made up of people who truly want people to dream big dreams and then it supports those people in having their dreams, come true.

If you are a person with big dreams and are also a person who would love to support others in achieving their big dreams, then the network marketing business is definitely a business for you. You can start your business part-time at first, then as your business grows, you can help other people start their part-time business. A business and people who help others have their dreams come true is a value worth working for.

Suggested Listening

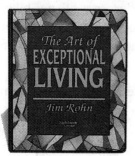

6 Audiocassettes
The Art Of Exceptional Living
by Jim Rohn

Nightingale Conant

NETWORK 7

Value #6: What Is the Value of a Network?

In 1974, while working for the Xerox Corporation in Hawaii, I was having a difficult time selling a product known as the Xerox telecopier. I was having trouble selling the telecopier because it was a new product. Not only was it a relatively new product, a commonly asked question was, "Well, who else has one?" In other words, having a telecopier had no value without someone else having a telecopier...i.e. a network of other telecopiers. Today, most people call a telecopier a "fax machine." As more and more people began using these new fax machines the value of the telecopier went up...and sales became much easier. I spent 10 years struggling to sell these new machines, now every business has to have one. The telecopier, or fax machine, went up in value once it became a *network* of telecopiers.

Metcalf's Law

Robert Metcalf is one of the people credited for creating the ether-net. He also more recently founded the 3 Com Corp, which produces the popular Palm Pilot. He is also credited for defining Metcalf's Law, which is:

$$A\ Network's\ Economic\ Value = No.\ of\ Users^2$$

Stating it in simpler terms:

If there exists just one telephone, it really has no economic value. The moment there are two telephones, according to Metcalf's Law, the economic value of the phone network is now squared. The economic value of the network would go from 0 to 4. Add a third phone, the economic value of the network is now 9. In other words, the economic value of a network goes up exponentially, not arithmetically.

Old Economy Versus New Economy

The power of Robert Metcalf's Law is more apparent when you compare an old economy company with a new economy business. AOL (America On Line) is a new economy business with literally millions of businesses and people in their network. Because AOL has a large network, the stock market values this company much higher than an old economy business...and because it is valued higher, AOL had the economic power to buy Time Warner, an older, more established, but old economy business.

Authors note: Time Warner Trade Publishing is the publisher of the Rich Dad series of books. I mention this because although Time Warner may be classified as an old economy business, it remains a great and progressive company to be a partner with.

Rugged Individual Versus Networker

During my father's generation, it was people like John Wayne who were the movie heroes of the day. In business, the heroes were business giants such as John D. Rockfeller and J.P. Morgan. These were men who built giant business empires. These men were much like John Wayne, strong, independent...rugged individuals. This model of businessperson continues to be alive and well today.

Yet, in the 1950s, new types of business models and business person's began to emerge. One of these business models is known as the franchise. A franchise is a form of business network, a network made up of multiple business owners working together. When franchises first appeared, many old-style businesses criticized them, some even calling them illegal.

Today, we all know, a McDonald's franchise owner has much more horsepower than the rugged individual who starts his or her own hamburger stand. If a McDonald's locates near the rugged individual's independent hamburger stand, chances are, the rugged individual is soon out of business.

As in any new business startup, a new franchise is not very valuable until it has more and more franchisees. I remember seeing the first Mail Boxes Etc. and wondering what it was. Suddenly, the company had explosive growth through adding franchises. In just a few years, I went from wondering what it was to seeing one every few miles. This is another example of Metcalf's Law at work.

In my neighborhood, a small packaging and mail shop that had been in business for years was forced out of business when a Mail Boxes Etc. franchise opened up in the same shopping center. Again, the rugged individual loses to the networker.

The Second Type of Networked Business

The second type of networked business is today known as network marketing. Instead of a network of franchised businesses, it is a network of franchised individuals. This second type of networked business came under much criticism at the beginning and continues to be criticized. Yet the industry continues to grow into many domains once controlled by traditional business. The reason the industry continues to grow is due to the power found in Metcalf's Law.

An Opportunity for Everyone to Harness the Power of Metcalf's Law

The beauty of network marketing is that it has made available to the average individual, people like you and me, the power of Metcalf's Law...but you must obey the law. If you follow the principle of the law, just joining a network marketing company is a good start, but just joining does not entitle you to harness the power. It would be like your buying a telephone, but you are the only one with the telephone.

In order for you to harness the power, your job is to clone or duplicate someone just like you. The moment there are two of you, your economic value is squared. The value of your network has just gone from 0 to 4. The moment there are three of you, the economic value of your network goes from 4 to 9. If the two people you bring in also develop two more people each, the economic value of your network begins to look like a rocket taking off for the moon. Instead of working hard arithmetically, your economic value begins to grow exponentially. That is the power and the value of a networked business.

In my opinion, working hard to build a network makes more sense than working hard as an individual. Imagine the difference between how many rocks you could carry by yourself from point A to point B and how many rocks nine of you could carry from point A to point B. Even if you only earn 10% of what the other eight are doing, it is 80% you earn with NO effort on your part.

In the long run, a successful networker has the potential to out-earn most professional people, such as doctors, lawyers, accountants, and other rugged individuals. The difference and the power are explained through Metcalf's Law...a very important value of a network marketing business.

The Future of Networking

You may notice that big independent businesses are now also beginning to network. It is why it made sense for Time Warner to join forces with AOL. The power of these two incredible companies networked together has the potential to create an awesome power in the world of business.

The World Wide Web, a.k.a. the Internet, is shaking up the world of business. The Internet allows more and more businesses and people to work as a network. Information can now be communicated instantly through the Internet. There will always be rugged individuals in the world of business, but I predict that the future is much brighter and more profitable for businesses and individuals choosing to work as a network.

Suggested Listening

6 Audiocassettes
Making Money on the Web
by Seth Godin

Nightingale Conant

Value #7: How Your Values Determine Your Reality

"So why are values so important?" I was asked in a class I was teaching on starting and building a business.

Realizing the question was important, I took my time answering it. After a moment of thought, I answered by saying, "Because our values determine our realities."

A hand went up and the next question was, "How does that happen?"

My reply was, "If people value job security, then the chances are that their reality is the reality of the E quadrant. They look at the world from the E quadrant and wonder why some people own the business they work for, while they are employed by the business. Many people fail to realize that their core values determine their reality. They cannot see the core values of the person in the B quadrant, the person they work for, because values are invisible. But the values between people in the different quadrants are different."

The person who asked the question sat silently and finally said, "Oh."

Continuing, I said, "And people who value being rugged individuals or doing things on their own, or who like to be specialists, will generally have the reality of a person from the S quadrant. They will say to themselves, 'If you want it done right, do it yourself.' Or they say, 'I just can't find good employees, people who want to work these days.' "

I looked out at the sea of adult students sitting in front of me, and I realized that most were analyzing their own core values.

"So if people don't change their values, they may have a difficult time changing quadrants," said the person who asked the original question.

"That is my reality," I said with a slight laugh. "At least that makes some sense to me. If your core value is job security, it is tough to become a B quadrant person, a person who values freedom. As I said, a B quadrant person does very little simply because he has other people working for him. An S quadrant person has a tough time being a B quadrant person simply because he doesn't trust other people to do a job as well as he can do it. So that person's core values determine his realities. If you value job security or don't trust other people to do a job better than you, then those core values form your reality of the world."

A young attorney raised his hand and said, "Because I think that I am the only one that can do my job, then I am the only one that can do my job. Is that what you mean by my values determine my reality?"

"That is a good example," I replied. "A good B quadrant person is always looking and finding people who are smarter than he is. When he finds someone smarter, then he is free to do other things. You on the other hand are working harder, doing a great job, and because you do a great job, more and more clients refer their friends to you. The problem is, each new client wants only you. So you work harder and harder, earn more and more, but ultimately there is a limit to your earning simply because in your mind, no one else can do what you can do."

The young attorney sat there silently, letting what I had just said sink in. Finally he said, "So being an S quadrant attorney limits my earning power because my time is a finite resource. If I shifted to being a B quadrant attorney, I would have to change my core values and begin to trust others to do a better job than I do."

"You've learned well," I replied with a grin. "The only hard part now is coming to grips with your core values."

"But if they are smarter than I am, then why do they need me?"

asked the attorney.

"Sounds like your core values talking now," I said with a grin. "It is that doubt that powers your core values and hence your reality. Since you fear people smarter than you not needing you, then you continue becoming smarter, which again traps you. And since you have to be the smartest, it is hard to trust someone else you feel may not be as smart as you to do the work. Smart people like you are often trapped in your own little world of needing to be smarter and smarter. You may recall I said the S in S quadrant also stood for *smart*. And that is why the S quadrant is filled with smart people like you, while the B quadrant is filled with the dummies like me. When my schoolteachers told me I was stupid, I decided that I should make being stupid my advantage in life. You made being smart your advantage in life...and hence we have different realities and work out of different quadrants."

"And that is why you do well in the B quadrant and I work hard in the S quadrant," laughed the attorney. "So I need to change my core values before I can become an attorney in the B quadrant."

"Makes sense to me," I said. "If I disagree with someone, it is often a disagreement on core values. And that is why I often hear people say to me 'Business is risky.' Or 'It's hard to find competent help today.' Or people argue with me saying, 'You can't make 1000% return on your investment in a month.' When I hear such emotionally charged statements, I know I am generally listening to a core value that has been disturbed. That is why values are so important when considering a change of quadrant."

"So when someone says 'Starting a business is risky.' That person is often speaking from his personal values, in this case the value of feeling secure."

Nodding my head, I replied, "That has been my experience." Thinking for a moment, I continued, saying, "I hear people say 'Starting a business is risky.' I hear this statement all the time. When I ask them what they do for a living, most of them are employees or are self-employed. The idea of starting a business or risking money as an investor shakes their core values."

A hand shot up from the back of the room. "But isn't starting a business risky? Isn't it a fact that most businesses fail in the first five years?" There was a strong sense of panic in the tone of this person's voice.

"Sounds like a core value talking," I replied.

"But it is true," the person demanded. "The facts are that 95% of all new businesses fail in the first five years."

"Yes those are the facts," I replied. "And all I am saying is that right now I believe it is your core value talking."

"But facts are facts," shouted the person. "I paid to attend this class on starting a business, and you have not told me how to overcome the facts. All you have been talking about for the last 20 minutes is some rubbish on core values and realities."

"So repeat for me the facts again," I said calmly, not wanting to rile this person any more.

"The facts are that 95% of the people moving from the E to the B quadrant fail in the first five years. I came to hear how not to fail. I don't want to hear about values."

Taking a deep breath I said, "I agree with your facts. But what you fail to see is that 5% of the new companies do make it. People with a strong core value of security often see only the 95% that fail and fail to see the 5% that make it."

"So how do I make it without being the 95% who fail?" asked the person, who was now beginning to cool down a little.

"By changing your core value," I replied. "Your core value of job security only allows you to see the 95% that don't make it. That is your reality. It is a reality of seeing only the risk and the failures."

"And you see the people who make it?" asked the person, who was again becoming a little agitated and argumentative.

"Yes," I said. "I can see Bill Gates, founder of Microsoft, and Anita Roddick, founder of The Body Shop. I can see the people of the world who made it. And seeing what they have is worth the 95% risk."

"Well it is easy for you to say because you made it," argued the person. "You are part of the 5% who make it."

"Yes I did," I said. "But I made it because I was also willing to be part of the 95% who do not make it. If you read *Rich Dad's CASHFLOW Quadrant*, the opening chapter is about my wife and I being homeless for three weeks. We were homeless because I did not make it. I was part of the 95% statistic twice before I made it. Today, I continue to be part of the 95% statistic of those who do not make it. Several of my B quadrant business ventures have recently failed. I have lost millions of dollars of my money and my investors' money...but I never lose sight of the 5% who do make it. That is my reality. I focus on the 5% who make it and that vision pulls me across the great abyss of the 95% who do not make it. The people who make it to the B quadrant have the ability to see the 95% as well as the 5%. The people who value job security can only see the 95% failure rate."

"But don't you hate failing? Isn't it a terrible feeling?" asked the person, who was now a little more subdued.

"More than most people," I said. "I hate failing so much that I use it as a motivation to move forward. When I lost my first two businesses, I felt terrible for a long time. Suddenly I realized that feeling sorry for myself only held me back. I took the pain of losing and began making corrections to my life. I began to study and find out what caused my losing. I used the pain of losing as my reason to win. My rich dad then said to me, "Losers use losing as an excuse to continue to lose. Winners use losing as the reason to win." He also said, "The biggest losers in the world are people who avoid losing." He also said, "You can always tell a loser who has lost. They are the ones who tell you why you won't make it, or why what you are doing is too risky."

"So how do you handle risk?" asked the person.

"Risk is part of learning," I said. "Risk is part of living. Every day that we climb into our car and drive down the road, there is risk...very big risk. When I was a little boy, my neighbor's father left for work one morning and never came back. He was killed in a four-car collision just a few blocks from home. Yet in spite of such grave risk, people continue to drive. People who avoid risk also avoid life and learning."

"So why would you bring up something so horrible as your neighbor dying?" asked the person who was still arguing with me about risk.

"Because moving to the B quadrant and getting rich is a lot less risky than driving a car or riding a bicycle," I said. "Yet depending upon your core values, getting rich can appear to be much more risky to your life than driving a car. The driving from one quadrant to another takes place inside of you. Driving a car from home to work takes place *outside of you*...and that is really risky, even if you are a good driver."

What Is Behind Your Core Values?

The class was nearly over. We had about 10 minutes to go. The person heatedly discussing the 95% failure rate of businesses was not convinced. There were others in the class also not convinced. I could see that this day's lesson on people's core values determining their reality had struck a chord for some...and the chord that was struck was not sounding a happy tune in their head.

A student who had sat quietly through most of this class, suddenly raised her hand and said, "So if values determine reality, then what determines a person's values?"

"Very good question," I replied with a smile. "I was hoping someone would ask the question." Turning to the flip chart, I drew the diagram of the Learning Pyramid.

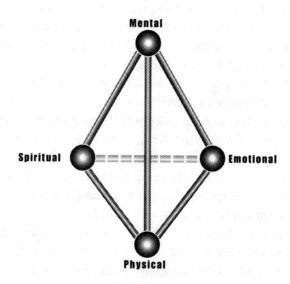

Turning to the group, I said, "As I said earlier, for there to be true life-changing education, the educational process must affect the person on all four points of the learning pyramid. For example, it is impossible to learn to drive a car without physically driving a car."

"Is learning to drive a car much like learning to change quadrants?" asked a participant.

"Yes...it is the same process," I replied. "Just let me point out what the differences are behind core values. Let us say you were terrified of driving a car. What values would that fear generate? What would you mentally think and what would you do physically?"

The class thought for a while. Finally one student said, "If I was really terrified of driving a car, I would tend to stay at home more. I would think that driving was risky, and I would tune into all the traffic accidents reported on television. Seeing all the accidents reported on the evening news would further justify my staying at home and watching more TV and seeing all the horrible traffic accidents."

"Thank you," I said. "That was a very good description." Looking at the entire class, I then said, "So how many of you want to live your lives that way?"

No one raised a hand.

"So let me ask you the next question," I said with a grin. "How many of you love driving even though it is risky?"

Hands shot up all over the room.

"How many of you have driven on a long, winding, empty road, along a beautiful coastline, or through beautiful mountains, and felt a high, almost spiritual feeling?"

Again, hands shot up all over the room. One participant, a young woman, jumped to her feet and shouted out, "Last summer, I took my little red sports car, with the top down, and drove along the ocean from L.A. to San Francisco. It was one of the best experiences of my life."

Another person raised his hand and said, "I just drove my family through back roads of the Rocky Mountains. It was as if we were driving through heaven."

Although there were many more hands still in the air, I thanked those who had shared their experiences of driving and turned to my diagram. Time was now up and it was time to adjourn. Pointing to the Learning Pyramid I said, "For people who value job security, the energy behind that value comes from the emotional point of the Learning Pyramid."

A hand shot up in the air and the person said, "You mean behind a person's values are his or her emotions?"

"Not all the time," I said. "In the case of a person who values job security, I would say that the emotion of *fear* determines that

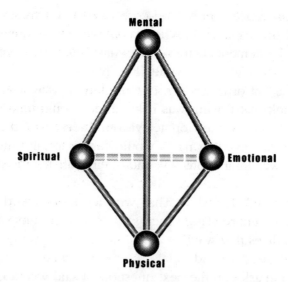

value, which in turn determines his or her reality. As an over-exaggeration, a person terrified of leaving job security is much like a person terrified of driving who then sits at home and watches the news of all the terrible crashes."

"Does the emotion of fear also drive the core value of the S quadrant?" another person asked.

"In many cases it does," I replied. "But it is a different kind of fear. It is the fear known as the lack of trust. These people often trust only themselves...or only people who have proven their trust to them. It is this fear caused by the lack of trust that keeps them, the rugged individuals, not trusting too many people, doing things on their own. It is this lack of trust of other people that creates their reality. In many cases it limits their earning potential just as job security limits the earning potential of the E quadrant person. Just remember that these are very broad generalizations. This is not an exact science. We are all wired differently, and we all respond differently to different situations. All of us have experienced fear and distrust. Different people just respond differently to these emotions."

A student stood up and said, "So are you saying that my emotions of fear and lack of trust are behind my core values? My emotions are keeping me stuck in the S quadrant?"

"Well, only you can answer that question," I replied. "As I said, this is not an exact science and each of us is different. After this class is over, I recommend you take some time to sit quietly and ask yourself that question. Come up with your own private and personal answers."

The student remained standing, thinking about what I had just said. Not satisfied with my answer, he then asked, "So what emotions are behind your core values in the B and I quadrant?"

"That is the question I have been waiting for," I said. "Once I answer this question, the class is over. It is then up to you to think about your own answers and your own values."

"So what is your answer?" shouted a student who had been trying to leave for the past 15 minutes. He was standing at the door of the class but could not leave until he had the answer.

"My answer is, what drives my core values in the B quadrant are not found on the Emotional Point of the Learning Pyramid. For me, the energy behind my core values in the B quadrant is found on the Spiritual Point of the Pyramid."

"The Spiritual Point?" the student standing in the doorway asked. "How is that possible?"

"Because the Emotional Point and the Spiritual Point are opposite," I said. "For example, instead of job security, I seek freedom. Freedom is a very spiritual ideal, and security is a very emotional idea or value. For people in the S quadrant, it is the fear of not trusting other people that keeps them trapped in the S quadrant. So again, it is the emotion of fear that determines that core value. Trust on the other hand, is a very spiritual ideal. Trust, leads to freedom, while fear leads to being trapped."

The class sat quietly after that statement. The student who was preparing to leave returned to his seat. The student who had been the most skeptical then said, "So throughout all your business failures, what kept you going was the vision of freedom and trust in yourself and other people."

"That is correct," I said. "But more than a trust in myself and other people, I have a tremendous trust in what most people refer to as God. I remind you that I am not a very religious person...but I do have a tremendous trust in a God, a power far greater than anything I can comprehend. And because I have that trust, I have tremendous faith in my ability to succeed, regardless of how tough things get. There is a big difference between *belief* in God and trust and faith in God. My rich dad used to say, 'Many people believe in God, but very few people truly trust in God. If they trusted more in God, they would be less fearful and more filled with faith.' It was my trust in God, a higher power, that ultimately carried me across the quadrants."

"So even though your businesses *failed* twice, you never lost *faith*," said the once-skeptical student.

I nodded. Taking a moment to gather my final words, I said, "My rich dad said, 'Vision and faith go hand in hand. In order to have a vision of a brighter and better future, you must have faith. If your faith is weak, so is your vision. And if your vision and faith are weak, your future will remain the same as it is today.'"

Walking out the door, I thanked the class. Most continued to sit in their seats. Turning, I said, "I will leave you with my rich dad's words to me...words he said after my second business failed and I was broke again. He said, 'Always remember that your values determine your reality. But also remember that you can choose between *fear* or *faith* to determine your values.'"

Author's Note:

I did an audiocassette tape set called *Rich Dad Secrets* with Nightingale-Conant. It discusses the differences between fear and faith, security and freedom, failure and success. My rich dad's secret was that he was a man of tremendous faith...and it was his faith that ultimately carried him out of poverty and on to becoming one of the richest men in the state of Hawaii. My rich dad knew that he could never fail...and that was his secret. He knew that failing was part of the process of success.

If you are like me, and enjoy listening to educational tapes that educate as well as inspire, this audiocassette set is just for you. The beauty of audiotapes is that you can listen to them while doing other things and you can listen to them over and over again.

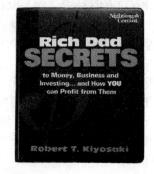

An Honor to Work with Nightingale-Conant

In 1974, I listened to my first set of audiotapes from Nightingale-Conant. Earl Nightingale's blockbuster hit, *Lead the Field* was a true gift to me. At that time I was working for the Xerox Corporation, gaining my sales experience and plotting my escape to the B quadrant. Listening to Earl Nightingale's tapes and other tape sets from his company have kept my spirit strong during the years of fear and doubt.

As you know, we all experience fear and doubt. The difference between successful people and unsuccessful people is what we do about that fear and doubt. Whenever I feel fear and doubt, I often find an audiocassette done by someone I admire, and I listen to that tape set over and over again. The process of listening to successful business people on tape is a way to bombard the Mental Point of my learning pyramid in order to strengthen the Spiritual point of my pyramid.

It had been over 26 years since I first listened to an audio-cassette of Earl Nightingale, when I got a call from the company he founded. The company, Nightingale-Conant was inviting me to do my own audiocassette set with them.

As I sat at their large boardroom table in their offices in Chicago, surrounded by audiocassettes of other great teachers, I said to the group seated around the table, "I am honored to be here today, but not because I am going to do a tape series with you. I am honored to be here just *because I am a student of your products.* If not for your library of educational products, I would *not be* sitting here today."

A Single Tape Made Especially for the Network Marketing Business

As you can tell, I am a strong advocate of lifelong education...especially education in the B quadrant. Because I support primarily the educational and personal development aspect of most network marketing businesses, Nightingale-Conant and I have done a single cassette tape especially for the network marketing industry. The tape is to be used as both an *educational tool* as well as an inexpensive *marketing tool* to leave behind with people you want to sponsor into your business.

If you are dedicated to your lifelong education, I suggest you include Nightingale-Conant as a source of B and I quadrant education. I did all the way back in 1974, and the value of their educational products lives on inside me today. I owe much of my success to their products, and I wish the same success for you. That is why I am honored to work with their fine organization.

Suggested Listening

6 Audiocassettes/Progress Guide or 6 Compact Discs/ Progress Guide Lead the Field by Earl Nightingale

Nightingale Conant

NETWORK 9

Value #8: The Value of Leadership

Each year, my dad would stand in front of hundreds of newly hired schoolteachers and welcome them to his school district. I remember as a little boy, watching him standing on stage, speaking with great confidence and sincerity. I felt very proud seeing everyone in the room sitting attentively and listening to my dad.

On many occasions, I also watched my rich dad stand and talk to his hundreds of employees at the company party. I also sat in the back of the room as Rich Dad addressed his board of directors and key investors, spelling out the past, present, and future of his businesses.

At a very young age, I realized the importance of one's ability to speak, but more than just speak, I realized the value of the ability to lead and inspire. After researching the education programs of many network marketing businesses, I noticed that one of the most important skills they develop in people is leadership. We all have this skill, but few of us are offered the training, the time, and the opportunities to actually develop it. Hence, only a few people ever truly develop this very important life skill. As my poor dad said, "Many people speak, but few people are listened to." And my rich dad said, "Money always flows to the leader. If you want *more* money, simply become *more* of a leader."

Leadership Skills Are Not Optional

My rich dad would also say, "There are leaders found in every quadrant. But you *do not* have to be a leader to be successful in every quadrant...except for the B quadrant. In the B quadrant, leadership skills are *not* optional." He would continue, "Money does not go to the business with the best products or service. Money flows to the business with the best leaders and the best management team."

If you look at the Cashflow Quadrant, there are leaders found in each quadrant.

My poor dad, for instance, was a dynamic leader in the E quadrant while my rich dad was a leader in the B and I quadrants. From a very early age, both dads stressed the importance of developing my leadership skills. That is why both dads recommended I join the Boy Scouts, play sports, and go into the military. When I look back on what training best supported my professional and financial success, I would say it was not the subjects I studied in school but the training I received in scouting, in sports, and in the military.

In the early 1970s, as I prepared to leave the military and enter the world of business in the B quadrant, I would hear my rich dad saying, "There are leaders found in every quadrant. But you do not have to be a leader to be successful in every quadrant...except for the B quadrant. In the B quadrant, leadership skills are *not* optional." I remember driving out of the main gate of my last military base saying to myself, "I wonder if my leadership skills will be good enough?" Those of you who know what happened to me after leaving the military already know that the leadership training I received in the scouts, sports, and the military was not enough for the challenges of the B quadrant business world that awaited me. One of the biggest values of a network marketing business is the leadership training you receive...a training that gives you the education, the time, and the opportunities to develop one of your most important business skills...leadership, necessary for success in the B quadrant.

Whenever I meet someone from the E or S quadrant having difficulties making the transition to the B quadrant, I often find someone with great technical skills, or management skills, but little leadership ability. For example, a friend of a friend came to me because he wanted to raise some money to start his own restaurant. He is a brilliant and well-trained chef with many years of fine dining experience. He had a unique new concept for his restaurant, a well-written business plan, great financial projections, a great location already selected, and a clientele that would follow him to his new restaurant, if he could just get someone to invest the $500,000 he needed.

It has been five years since he showed me his plan and I turned him down, as have many other potential investors. He is still working in the same restaurant as an employee, and he is still looking for the $500,000 in start-up capital. He has lost the original space because he could not raise the money, but he assures me he can find another location, if he could just get someone to invest in his dream.

Although everything sounds and looks good, I did not invest in his project. I do not know why the other investors did not invest with him, but I can tell you why *I* did *not* invest. It was not because I thought it was a risky investment or because I thought he would not be successful. I think his restaurant would be successful...but I still did not invest. The following are the reasons I did not invest.

1. Although he had experience, charm, and charisma, he

lacked the leadership skills to inspire confidence.

2. Although he could start a restaurant and run it successfully, I doubted if he could make it a big restaurant chain. His lack of confidence said, "I'll be successful, but I will always be small."

When you look at the CASHFLOW Quadrant, the difference between the S and B is size.

For example, if you heard someone say, "I want to open a hamburger stand on corner of 6th Street and Vine Street," you would know that this person would most likely be stuck in the S quadrant for a long time.

Now if you heard someone else say, "I want to open a hamburger stand on every major street corner in every major city throughout the world, and I will call this business McDonalds," you will instantly know that this person plans to open the same hamburger stand, but this person plans to do so through the B quadrant. In other words, it is the same hamburger business but from different quadrants. My rich dad would have said, "The difference in the number of street corners is the difference of leadership."

3. So I did not invest because I doubt if I would have ever gotten my investment back. Not because the business would fail. The reason I doubted that I would get my money back is because he would have probably always remained small, though successful. And if he did pay it back, it would have taken him a long time, and that violates my investor principles on how fast my money comes back to me. In other words, my money would be tied up in his investment instead of being reinvested in other investments. This concept is also called the velocity of investment capital.

The other reason I did not invest is because if he was to remain small, then why should I invest? I would be excited to invest if he was going to be big, and possibly turn my $500,000 into tens of millions of dollars. By lacking the leadership skills to make the restaurant big, it was doubtful that he could turn my $500,000 into millions of dollars. That is the price of lacking the leadership skills to take a business from the S quadrant into the B quadrant. As my rich dad said, "Money *does not* go to the business with the best products or service. Money flows to the business with the best leaders and management teams."

4. The fourth reason for not investing with him was because he had to be the smartest member on his team. He had an ego problem. As my rich dad often said, "If you're the leader of the team and you're also the smartest person on the team, your team is in trouble." What my rich dad meant was that in many S quadrant businesses, the head of the business is often the smartest person. For example, you go to see the doctor or dentist, not the receptionist, for your medical and dental needs.

In a B quadrant business, leadership skills are important simply because the B person has to deal with people who are much smarter, more experienced, and more capable than he or she is. For example, I saw my rich dad, a man without any formal education, deal with bankers, lawyers, accountants, investment advisors, etc., in order to do his job. Most of them had their master's degrees and some their doctorate degrees. In other words, to do his job, he had to lead and direct people who were far more educated and educated in many different professional fields. In order to raise money for his business, he often had to deal with people who were far richer than he was.

In many cases, an S quadrant person deals only with the client, peers, such as other doctors and lawyers, and then subordinates. In order to make the switch to the B quadrant, a quantum leap in leadership skills is often required.

To Him Leadership Was Optional

One day, this same friend of a friend called to ask me why I did not invest with him. I more or less told him the four reasons discussed above. Hurt and defensive, he said, "But I have the best training in the world. Chefs from all over the world dream of attending the culinary school I attended. I have years of experience, not only in the kitchen but also in managing the restaurant. How can you say I lack leadership skills?"

After a bit of patient explaining, saying to him that money, confidence, and leadership, go hand in hand, he began to understand my point...yet I think he still missed a lot. Finally he said, "But why do I need leadership skills when I have such a great education and years of experience?" When I recommended that he join a network marketing company that taught business education as well as leadership development, he got angry and said, "I am in the restaurant business. I do not need any more business education and leadership development." I realized that to him, lifelong business education and continuing leadership development were optional.

The Best Training in the World

As I stated at the start of this booklet, one of the most important values I found in some network marketing businesses was their life -changing business education. I also found some of the best business leadership development programs in the world. To me, the value of those programs is priceless.

Since doing my research, and dropping my prejudices against

the industry, I have met many successful entrepreneurs who received their business education in network marketing business. Recently I met a young man who made hundreds of millions of dollars from his computer business. He said to me, "I was just a young computer programmer for years. One day, a friend took me to a meeting and I signed up in his network marketing business. For years, all I did was go to meetings, attend rallies, read books, and listen to tapes. Today, I have hundreds of tapes and piles of books in my closet from those days. Not only did I eventually become successful in the network marketing business, but from what I learned, I soon quit my programming job and started my own computer business. Three years ago, I took my computer business public and made several hundred million dollars. I could not have done that without the training I got from that network marketing company. It was the best business and leadership development training in the world."

Leaders Speak to Your Spirit

In doing my research, I went to many meetings and large rallies. At these events I heard some of the best business leaders speak...speaking to inspire others to find their own personal greatness. As I heard many of these individuals tell their stories of starting with nothing and eventually becoming wealthy beyond their wildest dreams, I realized that the business was doing the same thing my rich dad told me to do...and that was to become a leader. I quoted him earlier saying, "Money always flows to the leader. If you want more money, simply become more of a leader." I realized that the best network marketing companies had educational programs that trained people to become leaders...not better salespeople.

When you look at the following diagrams of the Learning Pyramids, you will find two completely different communication styles.

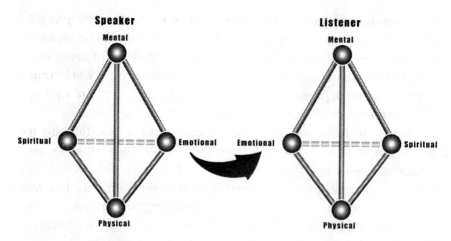

Speaking to the Emotions of Fear and Greed

Most people today, including our so-called leaders, often speak from emotion to emotion. They often speak from fear or from greed.

People who speak from emotion to emotion often say things such as:

1. "If you don't get good grades, you won't get a good job."

2. "If you don't come to work on time, you'll be fired."

3. "If you elect me, I will make sure you don't lose your Social Security benefits."

4. "Play it safe. Don't take unnecessary risks."

5. "Join my business. You can make a lot of money."

6. "Let me show you how to get rich quick."

7. "Do as I tell you."

8. "As you know, the company is having a rough time. If you don't want to get fired, you'd best not ask for a raise."

9. "You can't afford to quit. Who will pay you as much as we do?"

10. "You've only got eight more years to retirement. Don't make any waves."

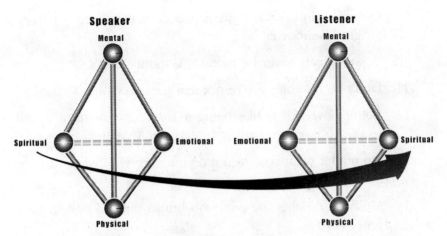

Speaking from Spirit To spirit

What a leader must do is speak from his or her human spirit and touch the other person's human spirit. That is a rare skill, especially today. And although rare, we often remember when true leaders speak...because when they speak, their words touch our souls and their words often go down in history.

You may remember some of these words that touched our souls and many are recorded in history.

1. "The time is near at hand which must determine whether Americans are to be free or to be slaves." George Washington

2. "Give me liberty or give me death." Patrick Henry

3. "Remember the Alamo." A Texas battle cry

4. "Four score and seven years ago." And also, "Am I not destroying my enemies when I make friends of them?" Abraham Lincoln

5. "You can't hold a man down without staying down with him." Booker T. Washington

6. "Ask not what your country can do for you..." John Kennedy

7. "I have a dream...." Martin Luther King

8. "Winning is a habit. Unfortunately, so is losing." Vince Lombardi

9. "Only our individual faith in freedom can keep us free." Dwight Eisenhower

10. "Cowards can never be moral." Gandhi

11. "Don't be humble; you're not that great." Golda Meir

12. "Being powerful is like being a lady. If you have to tell people you are, you aren't." Margaret Thatcher

13. "Do not let what you cannot do interfere with what you can do." John Wooden

14. "My best friend is the one who brings out the best in me." Henry Ford

15. "Try not to become a man of success but rather try to become a man of value." Albert Einstein

More than just offering the great potential to become very rich, many network marketing businesses exist to create people of greater and greater value. That is why I think some of the companies in the industry are priceless.

Suggested Listening

6 Audiocassettes/12-Week Leadership Mastery Plan/ Plus Bonus Booklet The Dale Carnegie Leadership Mastery Course

Nightingale Conant

NETWORK 10

Why the Network Marketing Business Will Continue to Grow

The future is very bright for the network marketing industry. There are economic changes coming and trends in progress today that will drive more and more people to the industry. The following are a few of these economic changes and trends I foresee.

1. **People want more freedom.** Gone are the days when people took a job at age 25 and stayed there for life...doing as they were told to do in order to keep their job. Today, people want to be more mobile, have more choices, and more freedom to live their lives according to their terms. A part-time network marketing business offers people more control over their lives and eventually more freedom. It provides a low cost of entry and readymade systems for those anxious to make a change.

2. **People want to be rich.** During my parents' generation, the rules said if you worked hard, the older you got, the more you were paid. You earned more money through incremental pay raises. And as you approached the end of your life, you would say, "When I retire, my income will go down." In other words, the assumption for my parents was that you worked hard all your life and retired poor.

Today, you have 25-year-olds who have never had a job but have become billionaires by building a computer software company. At the same time, we have 50-year-olds looking for jobs and hoping to earn $50,000 a year. What is worse, this same 50-year-old has little to nothing set aside for retirement and may never be able to retire. This 50-year-old does *not* need a job. This 50-year-old needs a way to get rich and provide a sustainable level of income for the rest of his or her life. Network marketing companies provide this opportunity by providing the education, mentoring, and business systems to assist this 50-year-old in building his or her own B business.

By the year 2010, which is not that far away, the first of 75 million baby-boomers in America reach the age of 65. Many will come to network marketing as a means of building that lifetime of security their job did not provide. On top of that, a person who successfully builds a network marketing business has the potential of joining the ranks of the ultra-rich of the world...far richer than highly educated professional people such as doctors, lawyers, engineers.... and far richer than many sports stars, movie stars, and rock stars. As the year 2010 approaches, many people who are already in a network marketing business will do exceptionally well as millions of baby-boomers come their way.

3. **Individual retirement portfolios will be wiped out.** Never in the history of the world have so many people bet their retirement years on the stock market. This is a recipe for financial disaster.

During my parents' generation, the retirees counted on the company they worked for and the federal government to provide the income stream for their retirement years. In other words, they did not have to worry about managing their retirement portfolio because the company they worked for did that for them.

Once you retire today, you are more often than not on your own. Millions of Americans have 401ks or similar retirement accounts, and that is all they have. If their 401k runs out of money, let's say at age 78, the retiree cannot turn back to their former employer and ask for help.

By the year 2010, there is also a strong possibility that the U.S. stock market may collapse, if it does not happen sooner. If the market collapses, many 401k retirement plans will collapse along with the market. If this happens, millions of people will never be able to retire or they will not have the pleasant retirement they dreamed of. Suddenly people with $2 million in mutual funds in their retirement account may find that their portfolio has been cut in half. On top of that, they may be stuck with a capital gains tax that could bankrupt the remaining value of their retirement portfolio. That is the risk of betting your retirement years on paper.

As I said, never in the history of the world have so many people bet their lives on the whims of the stock market. If this ever happens, millions of people will be seeking other sources for financial security, such as building a B business that a network marketing business can provide.

4. **More people will wake up.** As the year 2010 approaches, more people will wake up to the realization that the Industrial Age is over and that the rules of the world have changed forever.

In 1989 when the Berlin Wall came down and the World Wide Web went up, the rules of the world changed. Many economic historians state that the Industrial Age ended and the Information Age began. In the Industrial Age, the rules were that you worked hard and the company and the government took care of you. In the Information Age, the rules are that you had best be taking care of yourself.

As already stated, the year 2010 is an interesting benchmark because the baby-boomers will begin to retire in America. When that happens, chances are that the stock market will begin to deflate; if an accelerating deflation sets in as people pull their money out and head for safety, a panic may ensue, and a crash will follow. If people are wiped out financially, they become depressed, and if too many people remain depressed, it could lead to an economic depression. When the U.S. market crashed in 1929, it took nearly 25 years to recover. If you are 65 years of age when the next crash comes, you may not be able to afford to wait 25 years for the market to recover.

Why will it deflate? The stock market boom from 1990 to 2010 will be fueled by boomers spending money during their peak earning years and putting money into the stock market for their retirement. By the year 2010, that boom may turn into a bust...and with that bust will go many a boomer's dreams of a financially secure retirement. When the dream of a safe, secure retirement is gone, many people will wake up to the fact that the old ideas of the Industrial Age are over. I believe it will take another 10 years, i.e. the year 2010, before the masses begin to get the news. As more and more people get the news, the logic behind building your own business such as a network marketing business will make more sense. Until then, many people will believe the Industrial Age logic of work hard, retire, and let the government and business take care of you for the rest of your life.

5. **A world wakes up.** By the year 2010, as America's baby-boomers end the economic boom, a new set of baby-boomers will be rising up in Asia. As the economic boom shifts from America to Asia, people in international network marketing companies will be in position to move with this trend as their friends and neighbors fear being downsized. In other words, in the Information Age, the person competing for your job may not live in your town or in your country. In the Information Age the person after your job may live in Pakistan and be happy to work for $20 a day rather than $20 an hour, with benefits.

One of the problems I see with too many Americans today is that the boom economy has made many of us cocky and complacent. As my rich dad said, "When people come into a lot of money, they often think their IQ goes up. When people come into money, they think they are smarter but they begin to do stupid things. Instead of their IQ going up, their IQ actually goes down and their arrogance sky rockets." If you look at what happens to lottery winners or many sports stars who suddenly come into a lot of money and then are suddenly broke, you will see that my rich dad's statements have some validity.

I write these words as America's economic boom has dominated the world but the stock market has started to be volatile. The strength of the U.S. dollar has pushed the other currencies of the world down. As our income goes up, so does our personal debt. Never before have so many Americans been so deeply in debt. Many people have even borrowed money and put that money in the stock market hoping to get rich quick. Talk about arrogance versus intelligence. In other words, many Americans were getting drunk and partying long into the night because of this economic boom. As I write, the leaks in the economic bubble begin to show. Dot.com companies begin to collapse and stock investors begin to run out of high-flying technology stock and begin to seek shelter in more traditional value stocks. The volatility in the stock market today is being watched very carefully. When this boom comes to an end, many far-sighted people will begin to realize how smart it was for them to get into a network marketing business before the boom was over.

Sir Isaac Newton was wiped out in an economic bubble similar to the one we are currently in. Sir Isaac Newton is considered by many to be one of the world's smartest geniuses, yet he too was caught up in a financial boom known as The South Sea Bubble, which lasted from 1719 to 1722. He lost most of his fortune in the bust that followed that boom. In other words, even being as smart as he was, he was wiped out in the economic, get-rich-quick euphoria of that era. Once he had lost much of his wealth, he said, "I can calculate the motions of heavenly bodies, but not the madness of people."

6. **The bust may never come.** And maybe history will not repeat itself. And maybe today's volatility will stabilize and this economic boom will go on forever. And maybe those who look at the sanity of a network marketing business will be wrong. And maybe being personally responsible for one's life and financial well-being is wrong. Maybe expecting your job, the government, and the stock market to take care of you is the right thing to do. Maybe the best way to financial security is to borrow money and bet your financial future on the stock market. Maybe betting your future on luck rather than your ongoing education is the smart thing to do...but I don't think so.

As an American who travels the world, I see the problem with Americans is that we tend to live in a fish bowl. The world can look in but many Americans choose not to lookout. The world watches American TV programs. But how many of us have watched a TV program from India, China, or Korea? Too many Americans do not see how fast the rest of the world is catching on to the idea of Capitalism...even the Communists are becoming Capitalists today. Too many Americans have become soft, lazy, and expecting the life of a high paying job and easy money to continue on...and hopefully for them it will...but I don't think so.

Throughout history a bust has followed all booms. That news may be bad news for many people. Yet it can also be good news for others. One of the beauties of some network marketing businesses is that the world is your territory. If you have an international network marketing business, an economic bust can be just as good news to you as an economic boom. And if you can see all booms and all busts as good news, it is good news both to your soul and to your financial future.

These are just a few of the reasons I see the future of the network marketing industry only getting brighter and brighter.

NETWORK 11

Ask Your Sponsor to Teach You to Play

CASHFLOW® 101 and 202

As part of their ongoing educational programs, many network marketing companies encourage their people to play *CASHFLOW*. There are three different games in this educational series of board games I created to give people the same financial head start my rich dad gave me. The three games are *CASHFLOW 101, 202,* and *CASHFLOW for Kids.®*

These companies encourage the continual playing of these educational games:

1. To teach their people how to make a lot of money as well as keep the money they make. Too many people in the business make a lot of money and simply spend it all. *CASHFLOW* teaches people how to keep the money they worked so hard to earn and how to have that money work hard for them.

2. To have fun while learning and to discuss their dreams and economic futures.

3. To bond their business teams together around an educational tool. Many lasting friendships have been built around this game. Friendships begin because people have

something in common...in this case it is an educational board game that is designed to improve a person's financial future. Friendships begin when people realize that there are people in the world who are willing to help them achieve their dreams.

4. To introduce new people to the power of a network marketing business.

5. To change the way people think about money on the inside. My rich dad said, "If you change the way a person thinks about money on their inside, you change their world of money on the outside."

So those are just a few of the reasons many network marketing companies have adopted my *CASHFLOW* games. They have found the games to be fun, educational, team building, and a tool to introduce more people to their business. All you have to do is ask your sponsor to play the game. Even if you do not stay in the business, you will learn a lot about how to make more money and how to better manage your money and yourself.

NETWORK 12

The World's Best Mentors Are Ready to Guide You

I am often asked, "How do I find a mentor?"

My answer is, "There are many ways to find a mentor, and I have had many mentors in my lifetime. One of the best sources of great mentors I have found is in Nightingale-Conant's audiotape library."

In 1974, when I left the Marine Corps and joined the Xerox Corporation, I realized that I needed new leadership skills. The leadership skills I learned in the Marine Corps, while priceless and valuable, did not always work in the business world. In the Marine Corps I could shout, "Sergeant Jackson, tell the troops to report for duty at 2300 hours (11 p.m.)." Sgt. Jackson would reply, "Yes sir." And this is often after a full day of hard work. If I tried that in the civilian world of business, I would probably be sued for mental and emotional cruelty as well as have to pay excessive amounts of over-time.

Realizing that I needed more education and new role models as well as mentors, I came across Nightingale-Conant's audio-library. As I began my business and sales training with the Xerox Corporation, I supplemented my education with tapes from Nightingale-Conant. As I drove to work and to clients' offices, I would listen to these lessons by some of the world's greatest teachers, instead of listening to rock and roll music as most of my peers were doing. Today, I owe much of my success to the lessons I received from these great mentors on audiotape.

For those of you who are serious about your lifelong education, I highly recommend the audiotape library of Nightingale-Conant. Even today, I listen to their tape sets at the gym or in my car. In many ways, their library is one of the reasons why I slowly but surely became more and more successful as the years went on.

In Summary

These are the steps I recommend following, if you think a network marketing business is for you.

1. Decide to make changes in your life.

2. Start a Part-time network marketing business. Set a goal to stick with the business for five years, two years, one year or six months.

    My rich dad said, "The difference between a winner and a loser is defined by the finish line. Winners do not care if they come across the finish line in first or last place. All they care about is crossing the line. Losers quit before winning. Losers run 95 yards of a 100-yard race every day of their life."

3. Stick to the goal. Once you have made your decision, do not do what unsuccessful people do...which is to change their minds once they have made up their minds. If you decide to stay with the business for let's say a year, then for that year attend every event your sponsor recommends. You want to begin to improve your core thinking and values. I found that after the fifth meeting, my mind was finally beginning to change and I could begin to see things I could not see before.

4. Define the goal. Do you want to:

   Just earn a few more dollars a month?
   Replace your job's income?
   Become rich, which is $1 million a year?
   Become ultra-rich, which is at least $1 million a month?

5. Study as if your life depended upon it...because it does.

6. Dream big...and never lose sight of your dream. Even if you never achieve the dream, it is far better to have a big dream and go for the dream, than to dream small and achieve a small dream. As my rich dad said, "The difference between a successful person and a very successful person is the size of his or her dreams."

So regardless if you decide to pursue a future in a network marketing business...keep dreaming big dreams. Who knows, maybe someday your dreams will come true...so they might as well be big ones!

Thank you,
Robert Kiyosaki

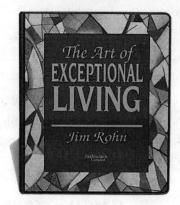

- Gain the respect and admiration of others using little-known secrets of America's most successful leaders.

- Get family, friends, and coworkers to do what you ask because they want to do it, not because they have to.

- Respond effectively when under crisis using proven techniques for thinking clearly and reducing anxiety under pressure.

- Recognize and develop talent in yourself and others while you learn to distinguish between image and substance.

And much more! Learn all the secrets of leadership mastery by ordering today!

6 Audiocassettes/12-Week Leadership Mastery Plan/Bonus Booklet entitled "Timeless Quotes on Leadership"　　　　　　*21110AY　$69.95*

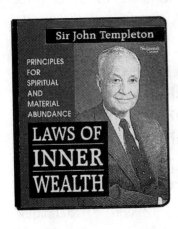

Discover wealth inside and you'll experience it outside!

How can I find inner peace in the midst of turmoil? How can I gain material wealth while maintaining my spiritual values? Fortunately, the world operates on spiritual laws, just as it operates on the laws of physics and gravity. In this enlightening and inspiring program, you'll discover the timeless and life-altering principles — the Laws of Inner Wealth — that will make your life richer, happier, more fulfilling and rewarding. Sir John Templeton, internationally acclaimed author, philanthropist, and investment manager, mixes ancient wisdom with science to reveal universal truths about your life and your highest calling.

4 Audiocassettes/Bonus Cassette　　16660AX　$59.95

Bootstrap your way to great success on the Internet!

Making Money on the Web. This revolutionary program will show you how to get your piece of the pie by "bootstrapping" — starting your own Internet company from scratch with almost no money down. Acclaimed Internet pioneer Seth Godin tells you how to outsmart the competition and cash in on the most important marketing medium since the advent of television. Act now and discover how to bootstrap your way to great financial success on the Internet!

6 Audiocassettes   *20850AX $59.95*

Profit from this classic "program of presidents"

Hundreds of thousands of people have profited from the wisdom and savvy of *Lead the Field*. In fact, it has often been referred to as "the program of presidents" because so many top executives have incorporated Earl's guidance and wisdom into their management philosophies. When you listen to this landmark program, you'll be awestruck by the simplicity and timelessness of Earl's words and ideas. You'll even learn the biggest stumbling block to high achievement — and how easy it is to overcome!

6 Audiocassettes/Progress Guide   *116-2AX $59.95*
6 Compact Discs/Progress Guide   *116-2CDX $69.95*

Be the person everyone wants to know!

In The *10 Qualities of Charismatic People*, Tony Alessandra offers a complete how-to guide to accessing and developing the kind of powerful personal magnetism that will draw people to you, make them feel comfortable with you, and compel them to help you achieve your personal goals. This dynamic program will teach you how to:

- Attract, inspire, empower, and motivate every person you come in contact with

- Project a powerful image of confidence, energy, and sincerity that will attract others

- Understand how to use physical space and time to your greatest advantage

- Discover the specific "image secrets" that all truly charismatic people know and use

- Much, much more

Once you unlock the power of charisma, you'll have an extraordinary edge in life enjoyed by only a select few.

6 Audiocassettes/Workbook/   *21410AB $59.95*
FREE Bonus Cassette

Nightingale-Conant
1-800-525-9000

CASHFLOW® TECHNOLOGIES, INC.

CASHFLOW® Technologies, Inc. and richdad.com, the collaborative efforts of Robert and Kim Kiyosaki, and Sharon Lechter produce innovative financial education products.

The Company's mission Statement is:
   "To elevate the financial well-being of humanity."

CASHFLOW® Technologies, Inc. presents Robert's teaching through books; *Rich Dad Poor Dad™, Rich Dad's CASHFLOW® Quadrant™, Rich Dad's Guide to Investing™,* and *Rich Kid Smart Kid™*; board games; *CASHFLOW® 101, CASHFLOW® 202,* and *CASHFLOW for Kids®*; and tape sets. Additional products are available and under development for people searching for financial education to guide them on their path to financial freedom. For updated information see www.richdad.com or contact info@richdad.com.

Rich Dad's
ADVISORS™

Rich Dad's Advisors is a collection of books and educational products reflecting the expertise of the professional advisors that *CASHFLOW®* Technologies, Inc. and its principals, Robert and Kim Kiyosaki, and Sharon Lechter, use to build their financial freedom. Each advisor is a specialist in his or her respective area of the B-I Triangle, the business foundation taught by *CASHFLOW®* Technologies, Inc.

Robert Kiyosaki's Edumercial
An Educational Commercial

The Three Incomes

In the world of accounting, there are three different types of income, earned, passive, and portfolio. When my real dad said to me, "Go to school, get good grades and find a safe secure job," he was recommending I work for earned income. When my rich dad said, "The rich don't work for money, they have their money work for them," he was talking about passive income and portfolio income. Passive income, in most cases, is derived from real estate investments. Portfolio income is income derived from paper assets, such as stocks, bonds, and mutual funds.

Rich Dad used to say, "The key to becoming wealthy is the ability to convert earned income into passive income and/or portfolio income as quickly as possible." He would say, "The taxes are highest on earned income. The least taxed income is passive income. That is another reason why you want your money working hard for you. The government taxes the income you work hard for more than the income your money works hard for."

The Key to Financial Freedom

The key to financial freedom and great wealth is a person's ability or skill to convert earned income into passive income and/or portfolio income. That is the skill that my rich dad spent a lot of time teaching Mike and me. Having that skill is the reason my wife Kim and I are financially free, never needing to work again. We continue to work because we choose to. Today we own a real estate investment company for passive income and participate in private placements and initial public offerings of stock for portfolio income.

Investing to become rich requires a different set of personal skills, skills essential for financial success as well as low-risk and high-investment returns. In other words, knowing how to create assets that buy other assets. The problem is that gaining the basic education and experience required is often time consuming, frightening, and expensive, especially when you make mistakes with your own money. That is why I created my patented educational board games trademarked as CASHFLOW.

Three Different Games
CASHFLOW, Investing 101®:

CASHFLOW® 101 teaches you the basics of fundamental investing, but it also does much more. *CASHFLOW® 101* teaches you how to take control of your personal finances, build a business through proper cash flow management, and learn how to invest with greater confidence in real estate and other businesses.

This educational product is for you if you want to improve your business and investing skills by learning how to take your ideas and turn them into assets such as your own business. Many small businesses fail because the owner lacks capital, real-life experience, and basic accounting skills. Many investors think investing is risky simply because they cannot read financial statements. *CASHFLOW® 101* teaches the fundamental skills of financial literacy and investing. This educational product includes the board game, a video, and audiotapes. It takes approximately two complete times playing the game to understand it. Then, we recommend that you play the game at least six times to begin to master the fundamentals of cash flow management and investing. **Price $195 US**

CASHFLOW, Investing 202®:

CASHFLOW® *202* teaches you the advanced skills of technical investing. After you are comfortable with the fundamentals of *CASHFLOW*® *101*, the next educational challenge is learning how to manage the ups and downs of the markets, often called volatility. *CASHFLOW*® *202* uses the same board game as *101*, but it comes with a completely different set of cards and score sheets and more advanced audiotapes. *CASHFLOW*® *202* teaches you to use the investment techniques of qualified investors-techniques such as short selling, call options, put options, and straddles, techniques that can be very expensive to learn in the real market. Most investors are afraid of a market crash. A qualified investor uses the tools taught in *CASHFLOW*® *202* to make money, when the markets go up and when the markets come down.

After you have mastered *101*, *CASHFLOW*® *202* becomes very exciting because you learn to react to the highs and lows of the markets, and you make a lot of paper money. Again, it is a lot less expensive to learn these advanced trading techniques on a board game using paper money rather than trading in the market with real money. While these games cannot guarantee your investment success, they will improve your financial vocabulary and knowledge of these advanced investing techniques.

Price $95 US

CASHFLOW, Investing for Kids®:

Could your child be the next Bill Gates, Anita Roddick of the Body Shop, Warren Buffet, or Donald Trump? If so, then *CASHFLOW for Kids*® could be the family's educational and fun game that gives your child the same educational head start my rich dad gave me. Few people know that Warren Buffet's father was a stockbroker and Donald Trump's father was a real estate developer. A parent's influence at an early age can have long-term financial results. *CASHFLOW for Kids*® includes the board game, book, and audiotape.

Price $39.95 US

Rich Dad's
ADVISORS ™

My poor dad often said, "What you know is important." My rich dad said, "If you want to be rich, *who* you know is more important than *what* you know." Rich Dad explained further, saying, "Business and investing are team sports. The average investor or small business person lose financially because they do not have a team. Instead of a team, they act as individuals who are trampled by very smart teams." That is why the *Rich Dad's Advisors* book series was born. Rich Dad's Advisors will guide you to help you know who to look for and what questions to ask of your advisors so you can go out and gather your own great team of advisors.

Robert T. Kiyosaki
Author of *The New York Times Best Sellers*
Rich Dad Poor Dad ™
Rich Dad's CASHFLOW Quadrant ™
Rich Dad's Guide to Investing ™
and Rich Dad's Rich Kid Smart Kid ™

Rich Dad's Advisors™ Series
Rich Dad said,
"Business and investing are team sports."

Each of us has a million dollar idea in our head. The first step in turning your idea into millions, maybe even billions of dollars is to protect that idea. Michael Lechter is an internationally known intellectual property attorney who is Robert Kiyosaki's legal advisor on all his intellectual property matters. His book is simply written and is an important addition to any business person's library.

Loopholes of the Rich is for the aspiring as well as the advanced business owner who is looking for better and smarter ways to legally pay less tax and protect his or her assets. It gives real solutions that will be easy to apply for your unique situation. Diane Kennedy offers over 20 years in research, application, and creation of innovative tax solutions and is Robert Kiyosaki's personal and corporate tax strategist.

Your most important skill in business is your ability to communicate and sell! *SalesDogs™* is a highly educational, inspirational and somewhat "irreverent" look at the world of sales, communications and the different characters that occupy that world. All of us sell in one way or another. It is important for you to find your own unique style. Blair Singer is respected internationally as an extraordinary trainer, speaker, and consultant in the field of sales, communication, and management.

Rich Dad's Advisors™ Series

Dolf de Roos is a real estate investor who bought his first property as an undergraduate student. After completing eight years of university education and earning a Ph.D. in electrical engineering, he was offered a job at $32,000 per year. The week before, he had completed a real estate deal worth $35,000. Consequently, he didn't accept the job, and to this day, has never had one. Dolf willingly shares his enthusiasm for real estate, and has "rattled cages" in audiences in over sixteen countries. He passionately believes that the "Deal of the Decade" comes along about once a week.

Own Your Own Corporation reveals the legal secrets and strategies that the rich have used for generations to run their businesses and protect their assets. Written in a clear and easily understandable style, *Own Your Own Corporation* provides the necessary knowledge to save you thousands of dollars in taxes and protect your family assets from the attacks of creditors.

About the Authors

Robert T. Kiyosaki

Born and raised in Hawaii, Robert Kiyosaki is a fourth-generation Japanese-American. After graduating from college in New York, Robert joined the Marine Corps and went to Vietnam as an officer and helicopter gunship pilot.

Returning from war, Robert went to work for the Xerox Corporation and in 1977 started a company that brought the first nylon Velcro surfer wallets to market. In 1985, he founded an international education company that taught business and investing to tens of thousands of students throughout the world.

In 1994, Robert sold his business and retired at the age of 47. During his short-lived retirement, Robert wrote *Rich Dad Poor Dad.* Soon afterward he wrote *Rich Dad's CASH-FLOW Quadrant* and *Rich Dad's Guide to Investing.* All three books are currently on the bestseller lists of the *Wall Street Journal, Business Week, The New York Times, E-Trade.com,* and other distinguished lists. Robert also created his educational board game CASHFLOW to teach individuals the same financial strategies his rich dad spent years teaching him . . . the same financial strategies that allowed Robert to retire at the age of 47.

Robert is often heard saying, "We go to school to learn to work hard for money. I write books and create products that teach people how to have money work hard for them . . . so they can enjoy the luxuries of this great world we live in."

Sharon L. Lechter

Wife and mother of three, C.P.A. and business owner, Sharon Lechter has dedicated her professional efforts to the field of education.

She graduated with honors from Florida State University with a degree in accounting. She joined the ranks of what was then one of the big eight accounting firms and went on to hold management positions with companies in the computer, insurance, and publishing industries, all while maintaining her professional credentials as a C.P.A.

As her own children grew, she was keenly involved in their education. She became a vocal activist in the areas of mathematics, computers, reading, and writing education.

So she was delighted to join forces with the inventor of the first electronic "talking book" and help expand the electronic book industry to a multimillion dollar international market. Today she remains a pioneer in developing new technologies to bring education back into children's lives.

"Our current educational system has not been able to keep pace with the global and technological changes in the world today. We must teach our young people the skills, both scholastic and financial, that they will need not only to survive but to flourish in the world they face."

Let Robert Kiyosaki teach you how to profit in both good times and bad.

- Robert Kiyosaki Live!

"My rich dad taught me the secrets to investing so that no matter what the market and economic cycles did, I would profit."

"I would like to teach you these fundamentals of investing at my upcoming seminar tour."

–Robert Kiyosaki, bestselling author, *Rich Dad Poor Dad*™

Now you can experience Robert Kiyosaki live during his seminar tours across North America.

At these events Robert will share the secrets that his rich dad taught him about the fundamentals of investing.

Robert Kiyosaki's message is clear: "Take responsibility for your finances or take orders all your life. You're either a master of money or a slave to it."

Find out when Robert will be in your area, by visiting:

www.robert-kiyosaki-live.com

Please visit our Web site, www.richdad.com to review:

- Additional Information About Our Financial Education Products
- Frequently Asked Questions (FAQs) About Our Products
- Seminars, Events, and Appearances with Robert Kiyosaki

Thank you

To Order Books Visit: www.richdad.com

North America/South America/Europe/Africa:
CASHFLOW™ Technologies, Inc.
4330 N. Civic Center Plaza, Suite 101
Scottsdale, Arizona 85251
USA
(800) 308-3585
Fax: (480) 348-1349
e-mail: info@richdad.com

Australia/New Zealand:
CASHFLOW™ Education Australia
Reply Paid AAA401 *(no stamp required)*
PO Box 122
Rosebery NSW 1445, Australia
Tel: 1 300 660 020 or (61) 2 9662 8511
Fax: 1 300 301 998 or (61) 2 9662 8611
e-mail: info@cashfloweducation.com.au